WITCHCRAFT IN AMERICA

Throughout our nation's history, people have been intrigued by the supernatural. The Indian medicine man, the witch doctor, the witch trials of Salem, Pennsylvania Dutch hex signs, Black voodoo queens and current interest in *The Exorcist* all testify to this abiding fascination with the occult. The author traces the practice of witchcraft in various parts of the country from earliest times to the present.

Books by
Clifford Lindsey Alderman

BLOOD-RED THE ROSES
The Story of the Wars of the Roses

A CAULDRON OF WITCHES
The Story of Witchcraft

DEATH TO THE KING
The Story of the English Civil War

THE DEVIL'S SHADOW
The Story of Witchcraft in Massachusetts

FLAME OF FREEDOM
The Peasants' Revolt of 1381

GATHERING STORM
The Story of the Green Mountain Boys

THE GOLDEN CENTURY
England Under the Tudors

THE GREAT INVASION
The Norman Conquest of 1066

LIBERTY, EQUALITY, FRATERNITY
The Story of the French Revolution

OSCEOLA AND THE SEMINOLE WARS

THAT MEN SHALL BE FREE
The Story of the Magna Carta

THE WEARING OF THE GREEN
The Irish Rebellion 1916-21

WITCHCRAFT IN AMERICA

Witchcraft in America

By Clifford Lindsey Alderman

Julian Messner New York

Published by Julian Messner, a Division of Simon & Schuster, Inc.
1 West 39 Street, New York, N. Y. 10018. All rights reserved.

Third Printing, 1975

**For Dawn Meaney,
because I like young people who like to read.**

Library of Congress Cataloging in Publication Data

Alderman, Clifford Lindsey.
    Witchcraft in America.

    SUMMARY: Traces the history of witchcraft in the United States
from its practice in the colonies to the present, including information
on voodoo and Indian witchcraft.
    Bibliography: p. 180
    1. Witchcraft—United States—Juvenile literature.
[1. Witchcraft]   I. Title.
BF1573.A42   133.4′0973   74-7586
ISBN 0-671-32685-6
ISBN 0-671-32686-4 (lib. bdg.)

Printed in the United States of America

CONTENTS

1 How the Devil Came to America 9

2 How the Devil Busied Himself in New England 19

3 New England Witchcraft Legends 31

4 Hechery in Pennsylvania 49

5 The Devil in Maryland and Virginia 62

6 Cunjering in Georgia 78

7 Satan's Mischief in Other Colonies 88

8 The Bell Witch of Tennessee and Mississippi 99

9 Voodoo in New Orleans 110

10 Marie Laveau, the Greatest Voodoo Queen 126

11 The Weird Witchcraft of New Mexico 137

12 Indian Witchcraft 150

13 Today's Witchcraft 169

Suggested Further Readings 178

Bibliography 180

Index 187

ACKNOWLEDGMENTS

Grateful acknowledgment for special assistance in the writing of this book is made to Paul P. Hoffman, head of the Archives Branch, Department of Cultural Resources of the State of North Carolina; to John Foster West of Appalachian State University, Boone, North Carolina, for permission to quote from his new book *You Take the Highroad: Along the Blue Ridge Parkway;* to Rebecca B. Colesar, archivist, State Library of the State of New Jersey; and to the always-helpful staff of the New York Public Library, especially the entire staffs of the American History and Local History divisions.

❉ ❉ ❉ 1
HOW THE DEVIL
CAME TO AMERICA

Witchcraft was practiced for thousands of years before it spread to America. Just how old it is no one really knows— perhaps as old as the world itself, if one considers the serpent in the Garden of Eden to be the personification of the Devil, father of all witchcraft and evil. Witchcraft was almost certainly known over three thousand years ago when Moses is believed to have written the Pentateuch, the first five books of the Old Testament of the Bible, which are also included in the Hebrew Torah. One of the laws given to Moses by God on the mountain and set down in the Pentateuch is the line: "Thou shalt not suffer a witch to live." And there are a number of other references to witches, sorcerers and other workers of so-called "magic" in the Old Testament.

There is controversy over the word "witch" as used in the Biblical line quoted above. Some authorities believe that the words were not translated properly in the ancient documents from which the Bible was put together. They say "witch" should have been "poisoner," but since poisoning was often used in witchcraft and because of the additional references

9

in the Bible to sorcery and other forms of witchcraft in the broadest sense of the word, it seems safe to assume that witchcraft in one or more of its forms was known and used then and probably long before that time.

Some authorities also dispute the inclusion of "magic" with witchcraft. One expert divides magic into "high magic"— that is, foreseeing the future by scientific divination—and "low magic," aiming to do evil, and thus associates the latter with witchcraft. But fortune telling, a form of divination, was one of the charges under which a witch could be accused and tried in the days of witch hunting. The one certain thing is that witchcraft is always intertwined with religion, even though religion so violently opposed witchcraft at the time when so many witches were persecuted, tried and executed.

Whenever witchcraft originated, presumably in prehistoric days, it spread in time all over the world. It came early to Europe. When in the seventh century Theodore of Tarsus was sent to England by the Pope to organize the Christian church that was eventually to become the Church of England, the Greek prelate signed a decree against those who destroyed people by spells, used the practices of witchcraft or made sacrifices to demons. The penalty was mild, however—one year of penance. But in the year 901 an early English king, Edward, decreed that witches should be banished from England. Later, King Ethelstan ordered death for witches under certain conditions. But there were few witchcraft trials, and these were handled by the churches, not the courts.

In the twelfth century many of the poorer classes in Europe became dissatisfied with the power of the Church of Rome and organized their own religious sects. Two of these, the Cathari and the Waldensians, became so strong that the

Church of Rome was alarmed. It struck back with the terrible Inquisition against the religious cults that opposed it, referring to their members as heretics. The purpose of the Inquisition was to root out and destroy heretics by questioning and torture.

Although the Inquisition denounced the Cathari as heretics, it accused them of holding assemblies to which they flew on broomsticks or on poles anointed with magic oil; of worshipping the Devil, who appeared at these meetings in the form of a hideous monster; and of seizing children, burning them and drinking potions made from the remains of their victims. All these things were characteristic of witchcraft, and in truth the Inquisition caused the death of thousands of accused witches.

The Inquisition gained new power in Europe in the fourteenth century. Ships from the Crimea, in the southern part of today's Soviet Russia, sailed to European ports with cargoes of grain, and with the grain came rats infested with bubonic plague, then called the Black Death. In the first three years that the highly contagious plague raged in Europe, it is estimated that one-third of the entire population died. In time the epidemic subsided, but every ten years or so it returned to carry off more of the people.

No one had any idea of how to treat those who fell ill of the plague or that the rats from the grain ships were responsible for it. The blame had to be placed somewhere, and it fell upon the Jews, who had already been persecuted for centuries. They were accused of witchlike practices in their religious services, including the eating of unbaptized children in their synagogues. In Germany, large numbers of the Jews were killed. Those that escaped fled to Poland and Russia.

The Church of Rome now considered witchcraft to be

heresy. Pope Innocent VIII issued a papal bull that gave new authority to witch hunters, and they made the most of it. The inquisitors struck in France and burned a good many accused witches at the stake; in Toulouse in the fifteenth century, four hundred people were executed in one day. But the worst witchcraft persecutions took place in Germany. No one knows just how many people perished there, but in Bavaria alone at least a thousand and possibly as many as two thousand were tortured into confessing that they were witches or sorcerers. They were then either burned alive at the stake, strangled first and then burned or broken on the wheel—a fiendish kind of execution in which the victims were lashed to a wheel with arms and legs outstretched while an executioner broke every bone in their bodies with an iron bar. In Würzburg, over a period of about ten years, there were nine hundred burnings.

It was not the Catholic Church alone that hunted down witches. Protestant religious leaders were equally zealous. The great Protestant reformer, Martin Luther, said, "I would have no pity on these witches; I would burn them all." And many accused witches were executed at the hands of the Protestants.

England and Scotland were both free of the Inquisition, but witch hunting raged in both countries from the fifteenth to the seventeenth centuries. In England, however, witchcraft was not considered heresy; torture was prohibited, and for a long time the penalties for witchcraft were mild. Thus witchcraft flourished there almost unmolested until the reign of Elizabeth I, from 1558 to 1603. Then an investigation of witchcraft in England was made, and as a result it was feared that even the Queen was not safe from the spells and enchantments of English witches. In 1563 an act was passed providing that "if any person or persons . . . shall use, practice or exercise witchcraft, enchantment or sorcery" in such a way as to kill anyone, the offender should be put to death.

Meanwhile, in Scotland, King James VI was intensely interested in witchcraft, and wrote a book about it. Under his rule in Scotland witchcraft suffered a reign of terror that was second only to Germany's in its ferocity. In fact, for fiendish tortures devised to make accused witches confess, Scotland had no rival. Witchcraft trials there continued into the eighteenth century, and while there are no exact records of the number of accused witches executed—usually after excruciating torture, and almost always by burning at the stake— one authority says four thousand is a reasonable estimate.

When Elizabeth I died in 1603, the Scottish King, heir to the English throne, became King James I of England as well as James VI of Scotland. He brought his witch-hunting ways with him and had a law passed against witches that was very severe.

The English witch hunts went on into the reign of Charles I, at which time a monster named Matthew Hopkins wrote a book, *The Discovery of Witches,* telling how witches could be recognized. It was so widely read that Hopkins took advantage of his fame by declaring himself "Witch-Finder Generall." He went about England ferreting out and accusing women of being witches. Town officials often hired him to come and root out these evildoers, and for two years Hopkins went from one place to another, always leaving behind him convicted witches dangling from the gallows.

At last an English clergyman, who, although he believed in witchcraft, nevertheless became convinced that Hopkins was sending many innocent people to their deaths. In 1646 he wrote a pamphlet denouncing Hopkins as a fraud. As a result the Witch-Finder Generall's grisly and profitable trade ended.

The American colonies were beginning to be well settled when the feverish hunt for witches in Europe subsided, though it did not completely end for many years. However, the newcomers to the colonies, for the most part, were lenient in their views of how witchcraft should be punished. Probably the horror of what had happened in England, Scotland, Germany, France and some other European countries was so impressed on their minds that the number of trials and executions was small by comparison with those of Europe, even when the smaller population of the American colonies is considered.

The exceptions to the general rule of leniency in witchcraft trials occurred in the Puritan settlements of New England, especially in those of Massachusetts Bay and Connecticut. There the stern Puritan ministers saw to it that the people lived and were governed strictly under the laws set forth in the Old Testament. They believed that "Thou shalt not suffer a witch to live" meant exactly what it said. The most notorious New England witch hunt was, of course, the Salem witchcraft delusion of 1692, but there were other accusations of witchcraft and other trials and harsh punishment, sometimes on the gallows.

Witchcraft, including sorcery and divination, took an endless number of forms, and so did the ways of protection against it. People from a number of nations settled in America, and each group had its own superstitions and beliefs. The belief that witches' power for evil depended upon a supernatural spirit whom some called Satan or the Devil, however, was universal.

There were also endless descriptions of this Chief of All

Evil when he appeared on earth. Satan might be a man or some other creature, especially a black cat or a goat. In human form he was usually a man of dark complexion, dressed all in black; he might be handsome, suave and persuasive; he might be awesome because of his flashing, evil eyes; or he might be a monster of frightful appearance.

At a fifteenth-century witch trial in Europe, the Devil was described as a being with a deformed body that was unpleasantly cold and soft and that gave off a foul odor. He was of dark complexion, was hairy and had horns and fiery, bulging eyes. Fire shot from his ears and there were talons on his toes and fingers. When he spoke, his voice was so terrifying that people would fall to the ground when they heard it, and sometimes go mad. Many descriptions told of the Devil's feet being like the hoofs of cloven-footed animals.

In other than human form, Satan might take the shape of almost any creature, most often a cat or a goat. It was believed that he often attended the secret night meetings of witches' societies, or covens as they are called. The meetings were orgies at which the witches danced all night; often "black masses," a mockery of the Catholic mass, would be held, worshipping the Devil. Sometimes the flesh of corpses stolen from graves or that of kidnapped and murdered children would be eaten, or the witches would drink the blood of a cat or some other sacrificed creature.

In order to work their devilish arts, witches had to have familiars, through which they obtained their power from the Devil. A familiar could be a dog, cat, goat, toad, bird, indeed almost any kind of animal, bird, reptile or insect. Old women were the most likely to be suspected of witchcraft, and any toothless, aged crone, often seen with a black cat or some other creature, was regarded with suspicion.

15

One sure sign that a person was a witch, according to European witchcraft, was a "witch mark." This might be a pimple, wart or some similar mark on the body, usually concealed from view; accused witches were always searched for them. Often the discovery of such a mark meant death for some miserable person accused of witchcraft.

Witches usually worked their mischief and always held their meetings at night. One widespread belief was that they flew or rode about the countryside in the darkness on horses stolen from barns, or on other animals. Many people believed that they rode on broomsticks or poles; in order to fly, witches would anoint themselves or their means of air transportation with a magic oil, ointment or potion.

Witches worked their deviltry in many ways, especially by putting enchantments or spells upon their victims. They used various methods of doing so, and such a curse might make the victim ill, bring him bad luck or kill him. A spell might be put upon someone by muttering the curse in his presence or even at a distance. Poisonous powders or potions might be thrown upon a person, put into his food or placed in his mouth or ears while he slept.

One thing about spells designed to harm or kill people always appears to have been true: the victim, in one way or another, was made to know that the curse had been put on him. In this way witchcraft used psychology; because the victim knew the curse was on him, his mind was literally poisoned by making him so afraid that he actually did fall ill or die.

One method of injuring or killing a person by witchcraft appears to have been used wherever witchcraft existed. The witch would make an image of the victim; it might be a doll made of rags, or a small, crude statue of wax. Into this image the witch would stick pins and thus, so it was believed, the victim was made to suffer from a distance.

Actual poisoning, usually believed to have been caused by witchcraft, was common. There are many deadly plants, berries and roots that grow wild, and the witch doctors were familiar with them and knew how to make fatal potions from them.

People naturally sought protection from spells, enchantments and other evil forms of witchcraft that might work harm to themselves, their families or their livestock and other property. One safeguard was to consult someone whose mystic powers were believed to be powerful enough to overcome an evil spell. Those who professed to be witches, witch doctors or sorcerers often made large sums of money by preparing charms, potions or magic incantations to break a spell. All sorts of ingredients and objects, often strange ones, were used. Some people carried charms against witchcraft on their persons at all times.

There was good witchcraft as well as bad. Witch doctors might devote all their time to healing those who were ill, using their expert knowledge of remedies made from herbs and other plants, though of course a certain amount of hocus-pocus to impress their clients went along with it. And witch doctors often profited handsomely by making love charms or potions, guaranteed to bring romance to the man or woman who bought and used them.

Sometimes the good ones were called "white witches," as opposed to the "black witches" who worked evil. Or a witch might work both good and evil.

The many forms of witchcraft practiced in Europe, Africa and other regions were bound to reach colonial America. Emigrants from Europe brought their own witchcraft beliefs, as did the Black slaves whose witchcraft originated in Africa. Witchcraft, coming first into Britain's American colonies, spread westward as settlement expanded. No part of the United States has completely escaped some form of witchcraft.

However, there was plenty of witchcraft all over what is today the United States long before the white men arrived. Since it is generally thought that the American Indians came originally, centuries ago, from Siberia by way of the narrow Bering Strait between that part of Russia and Alaska, the Indian form of witchcraft would have been Asian. As the Indians spread east and south through their new homeland, so did their witchcraft. All American Indian tribes had it and, though their beliefs varied in different parts of the country, there were enough similarities to indicate that most of these beliefs had spread from a single source.

The purpose of this book is to describe witchcraft in various regions of today's United States. English, German, Swiss, Scottish, Scotch-Irish, African and American Indian witchcraft existed in the colonial period and afterward, even right into the twentieth century. Hundreds of witchcraft stories and legends sprang up. Many are fanciful folklore with nothing more than superstition to support them. But a number are well enough supported by evidence and witnesses as to make them seem fairly believable. Some of these more credible witchcraft tales, fantastic as many of them are, will be told. So will the story of witchcraft itself in America, still flourishing to a degree few people suspect.

❋ ❋ ❋ 2

HOW THE DEVIL BUSIED
HIMSELF IN NEW ENGLAND

Strangely, the exposure and punishment of accused witches in Massachusetts is more famous than such occurrences in Europe, where thousands of so-called "witches" were put to death, largely by burning in the most horrible manner, during the sixteenth and seventeenth centuries. The witchcraft delusion in Salem, Salem Village and their vicinity was responsible for this notoriety. The story has been told so often that it need not be repeated here except in its bare details.

This is what happened: A group of girls in Salem Village, ranging in age from nine to their late teens, were supposedly tutored in witchcraft by a West Indian woman, Tituba, a slave in the home of the village minister. Apparently "bewitched," the girls began to go into mysterious fits, claimed they were being tortured and finally began to point out person after person as a witch or as one of the male witches called sorcerers or wizards.

Since at that time practically everyone believed in witchcraft, and apparently because two noted Puritan ministers of Boston, Increase Mather and his son Cotton, demanded that all the witches be hunted down and destroyed, scores of innocent persons were arrested, imprisoned and tried for witchcraft. Nineteen men and women were hanged, and at least one died in prison. One harmless but resolute old man who refused to plead either guilty or innocent, and thus could not be brought to trial, was killed under an old English law by having stones piled on him to force him to plead. He uttered not a word as the stones gradually crushed him to death.

It was not until people began to realize what a terrible injustice was being done in Salem that the witchcraft delusion ended. Executions for witchcraft in New England also soon ended. But before the Salem tragedy there were a number of them in the Massachusetts Bay and Connecticut colonies.

In Massachusetts Bay, Thomas Jones and his wife Margaret of Charlestown were tried in 1648. Thomas was acquitted, but Margaret, simply because of her skill in curing people who were ill, was adjudged a witch and hanged.

In Springfield, Massachusetts, Hugh Parsons and his wife Mary were tried for witchcraft in 1651. Both were found guilty, but Hugh's conviction was reversed. Their five-month-old son died during the trial and Mary, who seems to have been insane, confessed that she had murdered the baby by witchcraft. She was sentenced to be hanged, but there is no definite record of her execution, and she may have died in prison before they could bring her to the gallows.

Next, in 1656, Ann Hibbins, widow of a rich Boston merchant, was accused by her neighbors of being a witch. She was tried, but when not a scrap of believable evidence was found against her, she was acquitted. However, her neighbors, through jealousy or hatred, raised such a storm of protest that she was tried again by a higher court, found guilty and hanged (this was "double jeopardy," today forbidden by the Constitution of the United States).

Also in 1656, malicious neighbors accused Mary Parsons of Northampton of witchcraft. She was arrested, imprisoned in the grim, terrible jail in Boston and tried in that city, but the evidence against her was so weak that she was acquitted.

The Devil was busy in Connecticut as well as in Massachusetts Bay during the seventeenth century. There were a good many accusations of witchcraft and a good many trials, though fewer executions. The first known hanging of a convicted witch in New England appears to have taken place in that colony. Governor John Winthrop of Massachusetts Bay mentioned it in a brief line in his diary in 1647, not giving the victim's name: "One of Windsor arraigned and executed at Hartford for a witch." However, the woman's name appears to have been Alse (or Alice) Young of Windsor, who was hanged in Hartford on May 26, 1647.

The following year Mary Johnson of Wethersfield, a poor, ignorant woman who had a bad reputation in the settlement, was tried for witchcraft, confessed, admitted she had murdered her child and was executed. She was probably insane.

Little is known of the next case of Connecticut witchcraft beyond the names of the victims, John Carrington and his wife of Wethersfield. They were tried and found guilty in 1651, but not executed until 1653. This suggests that a good many people in Connecticut were already beginning to suspect that injustices were being committed. The magistrates probably postponed the Carringtons' executions in order to let possible public indignation subside.

Two other witchcraft cases in that year of 1651 may have had something to do with the magistrates' hesitation over the Carringtons' doom, especially since the events took place in Stratford, part of the then separate colony of New Haven, settled by Puritans, who were the most relentless of witch hunters. Goody Bassett of Stratford was accused of witchcraft and brought to trial in Fairfield. (Women of the poorer class in New England and other colonies were called Goodwife, often abbreviated to Goody, while their husbands had the title of Goodman.) The Puritan magistrates were determined to get information about other Stratford witches from Goody Bassett. They questioned her relentlessly and, as a result, Goodwife Knapp was accused and there was strong suspicion that Goodwife Staples was also a witch.

They brought Goody Knapp to trial and also questioned her at length, but she steadfastly insisted that the suspected Goody Staples was not a witch. So the vengeful Puritans hanged Goody Knapp. It appears that they were unable to find enough evidence to bring charges against Goody Staples, and also that, as a reward for her tale-telling, Goody Bassett was not hanged.

Another witchcraft case in Connecticut is notable because it is possibly the only one known in America in which the victim's son may have hanged his own mother. It involved Lydia Gilbert of Windsor.

Lydia and her husband Thomas had come to Massachusetts Bay from England in 1639 and until 1644 had a farm in Braintree, not far from Boston. But after the region along the Connecticut River including Windsor, Hartford and Wethersfield was settled, beginning in 1635, many people from towns in the Boston area migrated there. The Gilberts were among them.

In 1645 they bought land in Windsor from Francis Stiles and also leased some additional acreage from him. Four of the Gilberts' sons came along with them, but the two older ones went on to Hartford and settled there. Of the two older sons, Jonathan Gilbert became the marshal at Hartford, a position not unlike that of sheriff, which also put him in charge of the prison there.

In 1640 Francis Stiles sold his land in Windsor and moved to Stratford. However, he left his house with his brother Henry, who was a bachelor in his fifties. Henry was probably lonely after his brother left and was also no expert housekeeper or cook, and he invited the Gilberts to move in with him into his larger farmhouse. They accepted, and this turned out to be a fatal mistake for Lydia Gilbert.

For three years the arrangement worked splendidly. Although Thomas Gilbert was nearly seventy, he was still strong and active and was able to continue working the farmland he owned. Lydia kept up the Stiles house, cooked, sewed and mended for her family and Henry Stiles.

Henry was a member of the Windsor train band, a volunteer organization similar to militia which could be called out in case of an Indian attack or some other serious emergency. Now and then, training days were held during which the entire train band marched and maneuvered on the village green. Training days were festive occasions, with the whole village turning out to watch while drums thundered and fifes tootled. But the one held in Windsor in November, 1651, was a tragedy.

In some way Thomas Allyn's musket accidentally discharged during the maneuvers. The bullet struck Henry Stiles and killed him. There was absolutely no question that it was an accident, and when an investigation was held, Thomas Allyn pleaded guilty to negligence and was fined £20.

Of course, the tragic accident ended the Gilberts' stay at the Stiles house, since the property went to Henry's brother John, who moved into the house with his own family. The Gilberts bought a farm nearby.

Nearly three years passed. Then, without warning, certain persons in Windsor whose names are not known charged Lydia Gilbert with using witchcraft to "murder" Henry Stiles. It was all so foolish that it seems impossible to believe that any court would think Lydia had anything to do with Henry Stiles' death. But this was 1654, and the Devil was suspected of being up to mischief in both Connecticut and Massachusetts Bay through his willing servants, the witches of the two colonies. Probably Lydia had enemies in Windsor; she was an old woman and they were always apt to be suspected of witchcraft, especially by those who wished them harm.

The indictment against Lydia Gilbert charged that she "of late years or still dust give Entertainment to Satan, the great Enemy of god and mankind, and by his help she hath killed the body of Henry Stiles, besides other witchcrafts for which . . . thou Deservest to Dye."

In all probability, Jonathan Gilbert, as marshal, had to come from Hartford to Windsor to arrest his own mother and to take her back to prison in Hartford. There she was put into a dungeon. Prisoners in the dungeon were fettered either with chains or with the leg irons called gyves. The only light in the dungeon was the dim, flickering one from a lamp that burned grease. Some prisoners were allowed certain comforts, such as a feather bed, bolster, bed rug and blanket, and it is impossible to believe that Jonathan Gilbert did not see that his mother was furnished with these articles to make her imprisonment a little easier.

24

Lydia Gilbert came to trial, the jury found her guilty of witchcraft and she was sentenced to die. Neither the governor of the colony nor the General Court interceded for her. This miscarriage of justice, as terrible as any during the Salem witchcraft delusion, came to its conclusion when Lydia was hanged, probably on Hartford's public gallows, with the usual mob assembled for such spectacles to jeer and hurl insults at the wretched victim.

There are no recorded details of the hanging, so it is not known whether Jonathan Gilbert, whose duties included that of hangman, executed his mother, but it would seem likely that he got someone to substitute for him in such a dreadful task. Nevertheless, if the Devil was responsible for what happened to innocent Lydia Gilbert, he must have rubbed his hands in triumph at his victory over the forces of good in the world.

In 1662 something curiously like the Salem witchcraft delusion of thirty years later took place in Hartford. A teen-age girl, Ann Cole, began to charge her neighbors with witchcraft. The first ones to fall prey to these malicious accusations were Rebecca and Nathaniel Greensmith. Ann Cole submitted a long list of charges against them, and like some of those in the Salem delusion, Rebecca Greensmith confessed that she had submitted to the Devil's wiles when he appeared to her in the form of a deer and promised her a "merry meeting" at Christmas if she would serve him.

Rebecca next accused her own husband, Nathaniel, of witchcraft. She said first that a red creature had followed him in the woods. He explained that by saying it was a fox. But this woman he had supposed to be his loving wife had more incriminating testimony against him. Nathaniel, she said, although he was a small, frail man, was able to hew and put large logs in his cart and bring them home. Both the Greensmiths appear to have been executed. And as was doubtless true of participants in other witchcraft cases, Rebecca Greensmith was probably mentally deranged.

Next, Mary Sanford was accused, tried and executed. The rest accused by Ann Cole escaped the hangman's noose in one way or another. Judith Varlett might have been hanged if she had not been a relative of powerful and famous Peter Stuyvesant, governor of the then Dutch colony of New Amsterdam, who interceded and saved her. Four others managed to escape to safety in the Rhode Island colony. And unlike the Salem delusion, the Hartford one ended without becoming an epidemic. A woman in Farmington, outside Hartford, was executed for witchcraft that same year, but the case had nothing to do with Ann Cole's charges.

The 1669 trial of Katherine Harrison of Wethersfield seems to have been a clear case of malicious jealousy, simply because she had money. She had been a poor servant girl who had married John Harrison, the town surveyor and town crier. He had died, leaving her well-to-do. Doubtless as a result of her good fortune, she was very unpopular. Katherine's neighbors, according to a complaint she made to the court, had wronged her cruelly. Her oxen, cows, pigs and some of her horses had been tortured and some had had their backs broken. The neighbors got back at her by charging she was a witch.

Governor John Winthrop of Connecticut, son of the former governor of Massachusetts Bay, presided at Katherine Harrison's trial. The evidence presented by her vengeful neighbors was ridiculous. Because of her witchcraft, it was testified, a tailor in Wethersfield had been unable to make the sleeves fit to a jacket he was working on. The same witness had seen a calf riding in a cart; a little later, Katherine Harrison's magic changed the calf back into her own husband. The witness had gone to Mrs. Harrison and told her that he suspected her of being a witch. She replied that she would get even with him, and she did. He woke in the night to find her standing by his bedside, pulling, punching and threatening to strangle him. So said the witness.

The rest of the testimony was equally absurd. Mrs. Harrison's bees, said another witness, had flown away across the Connecticut River, but by some magic spell she had brought them back very quickly. A man testified that he had tried to graze his cattle on some of Katherine's land, but they ran away—which would seem to have served him right for pasturing the animals there, apparently without her permission. A woman had dreamed of Mrs. Harrison one night; the next morning her child was sick. It was also said that Katherine spun finer yarn than anyone else, a sure sign of witchcraft. And she told fortunes, something done only by witches.

The jury seems to have swallowed all this nonsense, for they convicted Katherine Harrison. But she had stoutly defended herself, and some of the magistrates, who seem to have had some common sense, disagreed with the jury. They decided to leave her fate up to the ministers of the colony.

Since Wethersfield and the nearby settlements along the Connecticut River had been founded largely by people who disagreed with the harsh Puritanism of Massachusetts Bay, the ministers were not as ruthless in their witch hunting as the Mathers and other Puritan ministers of that colony. At least they spared Katherine Harrison's life and generously

27

agreed that after paying all the costs of her trial and imprisonment, she might then leave Connecticut under banishment.

There were a number of other witchcraft cases in Connecticut; in fact, they extended well into the eighteenth century, the last one occurring in 1768. But by that time witch hunting had waned, perhaps partly because an old woman of Colchester, accused of witchcraft, brought suit against her accusers for defamation of character and was awarded damages.

Actually, except for the atrocity of the Salem witchcraft delusion, there were not a great many executions for witchcraft in New England. Rhode Island had no witchcraft trials, probably because of the benevolent government established by its founder, Roger Williams. With its complete religious freedom, it did not attract witch-hunting Puritans. New Hampshire did have some witchcraft trials, and some of the strangest supernatural happenings of all are supposed to have taken place there. There was a lack of witch hunts there before 1641, however, probably because there were few Puritans among the earliest settlers. But in that year of 1641, the colony was placed under the rule of Massachusetts Bay and remained so for forty years. Puritan settlers came to New Hampshire and immediately began to make trouble. Probably that is why the trial of Goodwife Jane Walford for witchcraft took place in 1656.

Several witnesses gave some weird and unbelievable testimony when Goody Walford's case came before the court of assistants in Portsmouth. One accuser, Susannah Trimmings, evidently a neighbor and perhaps an enemy of Goody Walford, testified that when she was going home one night she heard a rustling in the woods. She thought it was only swine rooting there until suddenly an old woman appeared whom she recognized as Goody Walford, wearing a white linen hood tied under her chin, a red waistcoat and petticoat and a black hat.

The old woman asked Susannah to lend her a pound of cotton. Susannah refused, saying she had only two pounds in the house. Goody Walford then said darkly that Susannah would be sorry, since she would soon depart on a long journey. With that, the old woman assumed the shape of a cat and vanished.

At that moment something struck Susannah; she described it as "like a clap of fire in the back." Her husband, Oliver Trimmings, then took up the story. He said his wife came home in a shocking condition. She could not speak and something in her throat was hampering her breathing. When he unlaced her clothes and put her to bed, she was able to cry, "Lord, have mercy upon me; this wicked woman will kill me." She added that her back was like a flame of fire and that the lower part of her body was paralyzed. Oliver said this last was certainly true, for he had punched her and she did not feel it. Furthermore, although Susannah was now better, she still complained of the aches and pains the wicked witch had inflicted upon her.

Another witness, Nicholas Howe, had a story oddly like the one told over thirty years later by a witness in the Salem witchcraft trials, who said one of the accused witches had appeared in his bedchamber although the doors and windows were shut, and then had flown out through a tiny crack in a window sill. Nicholas Rose said that Goody Walford appeared to him while he was in bed at night, made him speechless by placing her hand on his chest and then vanished. He was in great pain the rest of the night. A week later she paid him a second visit.

The assistants who were trying Goody Walford had more sense than the credulous magistrates in the Salem witchcraft trials. They discharged her with a warning to behave herself in the future.

The case was doubtless one of malicious spite against a neighbor, and although it was some years before Goody Walford got around to it, she finally sued her accusers for damages and was awarded £500 and payment of the costs of her trial.

❉ ❉ ❉ 3

NEW ENGLAND
WITCHCRAFT LEGENDS

There are dozens of New England legends that have to do with witchcraft or the supernatural, but many are just that—unbelievable tales that have sprung up in the minds of superstitious people. However, there are some that either have some basis in fact or are supported by enough evidence to make them credible, especially because these mysteries have never been solved.

Some of the strangest of these more plausible New England legends are supposed to have taken place in New Hampshire. One is the amazing story of Lithobolia, which is said to have taken place on an island in Portsmouth harbor.

In 1696, Portsmouth was, as it is today, a beautiful place. It stood on the rockbound, pine-forested New England coast, and since Maine was then a part of Massachusetts Bay, New Hampshire could claim to be the northernmost, in its entirety, of the American colonies.

The handful of men who had come from England in 1623 had chosen well in selecting the site for the colony's first settlement. The Indians called the region Piscataqua, meaning "the place where three rivers meet," for the Piscataqua River that widens and flows into a splendid harbor there is actually formed by the confluence of three streams. Those original inhabitants of New Hampshire also chose a beautiful name for their settlement—Strawberry Bank, because of the lush beds of wild strawberries that grew there.

Now, in 1696, the charming name had been changed to one that at least described its new importance in the American colonies—Portsmouth, the largest of New Hampshire's towns and the most prosperous, for it was an important seaport and shipbuilding center. Ships sailed from there to many other ports far and near. Merchant-shipowners were becoming rich. They were building splendid mansions that made Portsmouth a showplace.

In short, Portsmouth was a busy, thriving and peaceful town. It was the last place in which one would expect Satan to be at work. The suspicion that toothless, wrinkled old women might be witches had faded greatly once the terrible Salem witchcraft delusion of 1692 was over. Yet only four years later, in 1696, there was an occurrence in Portsmouth harbor that its citizens were firmly convinced only witchcraft could have caused.

Indeed, no reasonable explanation has ever come to light for the strange and frightening incidents caused by what the people of Portsmouth came to call Lithobolia, a Latin word meaning "Stone-Throwing Demon." Nor was the occurrence of these incidents unsupported by reliable witnesses. According to George Chamberlayne, himself one of the victims, who wrote the story of Lithobolia in 1698, eyewitnesses included the governor of Rhode Island, a former governor of West New Jersey, a merchant from witch-hunting Salem, another from Barbados and a ship captain.

The only person who was ever suspected of causing the mischief was an elderly woman who lived on Great Island in Portsmouth harbor. There was a dispute between her and her next-door neighbor, George Walton, over the boundaries of their two properties. The case was taken to court and a small piece of land claimed by both was awarded to Mr. Walton.

The resentful lady was heard to say that Mr. Walton should never quietly enjoy the ground that she felt had been stolen from her. Soon afterward, the trouble began.

In his account, Mr. Chamberlayne does not describe Mr. Walton's occupation, but he was obviously a well-to-do farmer who owned a comfortable house on Great Island, had servants, was a member of the governor's council and, as shown by Chamberlayne's story, often entertained notable guests. Chamberlayne seems either to have been a boarder with the family or to have rented lodgings in the upper part of the house.

It all started about ten o'clock on a Sunday night in July, 1696. Chamberlayne had gone to bed when he heard many stones striking the roof and sides of the house. He got up, hastily dressed and went downstairs, where the Walton family, also roused, had gathered. It was a bright moonlit night and all of them went outside, but found nothing.

Some of the barrage of rocks had penetrated the house, for one of Mr. Walton's sons had been hit on the leg and another on the thigh. When the searching party returned to the house, it was greeted by another hail of stones, some of them big ones. The main room downstairs was a shambles. Inexplicably, the window casements had been forced open, apparently from the inside, since they opened outward. Through them had come the second batch of stones. Brass and pewter objects, including a large pewter pot, had been dented and thrown to the floor. Two heavy candlesticks had been knocked off the table. A member of the family started to pick up one of the stones, but quickly withdrew his hand: the rock was so hot that it might have come out of a fire. Other rocks, though not all, were also hot.

They picked up some of the cooler stones and arranged them on the table to study them. Suddenly they discovered that two of them had vanished.

For four hours the bombardment went on. Chamberlayne finally went back upstairs to bed and managed to fall asleep, but a tremendous noise brought him bolt upright, fully awake. It was caused by an eight-pound stone that had smashed through his chamber door. He went back to bed, but almost immediately a whole brick came flying into the room. After that, the missiles abruptly ceased coming, and Mr. Chamberlayne slept until morning.

Then, downstairs, he found the servants in a turmoil. While preparing breakfast, they had discovered that the spit used for roasting meat had disappeared from the chimney corner, but almost at once it came whizzing down the chimney and embedded itself in a log. One of the family moved the log to the other side of the chimney corner, but as soon as he let go it flew out of a window. A pressing iron on the chimney ledge vanished and was found in the yard.

Chamberlayne had taken the big stone that had crashed into his bedroom and put it on the table there. A little later a loud noise brought him back upstairs, and he found that the stone had flown into the antechamber outside his bedroom. He picked it up and put it back on the table. The stone-throwing spirit evidently decided not to continue the contest, and the stone remained in the bedroom.

More stones crashed against the house that day. Meanwhile, Mr. Walton had gone into the fields with some of his hired hands. They came under the fire of the mysterious rock thrower there. A minister, a Mr. Woodbridge, had heard of the strange goings-on and came to see for himself. He, Mr. Chamberlayne, a neighbor named Clark and his son, along with others who had flocked to the scene as the news spread, saw more stones come hurtling through the air, but no trace of anyone throwing them. One woman declared it was being done by some boys at work nearby, and instantly her small son, standing by her, was knocked to the ground by a rock.

After supper that evening, before the summer dusk, Mr. Chamberlayne went to his room to play, as he often did, on a musical instrument (he does not say what it was). The door of the room was open and a big stone came rolling in.

That same early evening a clue of sorts turned up, at least to those who believed in witchcraft, which of course included almost everyone in those days. Two young men who were strolling through the fields and orchard saw a black cat. People knew that witches used toads, bats, dogs, birds, cats and other creatures as their familiars. A black cat was an especially favored familiar, and it was also believed that Satan himself often took the form of a black cat when he visited the earth to do evil. Considering the conditions at the Walton farm, the young men felt it best to be protected and had armed themselves. They shot at the cat, but missed, and it scampered out of sight. Here, at least, was some evidence that the Devil was about.

That same evening two girls, grandchildren of Mr. Walton, were standing by the porch-chamber window. They saw a hand stretched out from the hall window, as if throwing stones, but the only person in the hall at that time was Mr. Chamberlayne.

The next night, Monday, the servant maids were in bed in their room next to the kitchen when five or six stones smashed through the window. One girl was struck as she lay in bed. They heard a strange whistling sound that was also noticed by two of Mr. Walton's sons, who dashed out of the house, hoping to catch the mysterious culprit. They found nothing, but when they reached the back of the house they heard a light trampling, like that of a colt, yet nothing was there.

During the rest of the week the spirit seems to have tired of the sport, but the following week the torment began again. This time it took place at the house of Mr. Walton's married son, William, on another island in a part of the harbor known as the Great Bay. The elder Mr. Walton needed some firewood, so he rowed some of his hands over there, left them and returned to Great Island that night, presumably in a small rowboat.

The next morning, while the men were felling timber in the woods on the Great Bay island, a shower of stones fell on them. They gathered some up in a hat, but while they were carrying them to the boat, the hat disappeared. They found it later under a square piece of wood in the road. That same day the unknown hand tossed stones into young William's house and a half brick landed in his baby son's cradle.

The men had not finished their cutting and resumed it the following day. It had been hot when Mr. Walton rowed the men to the island and he had taken off a girdle he wore and left it in the boat. Both it and the boat's anchor vanished and were never seen again. Also, a setting-pole, used in place of oars to propel the boat in shallow places, flew into the water several times as the men were returning to Great Island.

Nothing much more happened until Friday of that week. Meanwhile, Mr. Walton had some distinguished guests who included, as mentioned, Samuel Jennings, former governor of West New Jersey (there were two New Jerseys, West and East, at that time) and Walter Clarke, governor of Rhode Island (Mr. Chamberlayne calls him deputy governor, but the records show that he was governor of the colony from January, 1696, to March, 1698). There were also the two merchants and the ship captain. According to Mr. Chamberlayne's account, these witnesses saw four or five hot stones thrown at the house the night they were there.

That weekend only a few stones were thrown, but on Monday night a furious torrent fell on the house, dislodging most of the pewter dishes and utensils from their places. Then, about midnight, the demon concentrated its rage on Mr. Chamberlayne. At intervals two huge rocks, each weighing about thirty pounds, smashed into his antechamber, knocking over furniture and causing pictures to fall off the wall.

Mr. Chamberlayne got out of bed, lit a candle and went into the anteroom. Stones and bricks by the score came shooting through two windows, breaking the panes and putting out the candle. A wooden mortar, always kept in the kitchen for crushing and powdering food, came from nowhere and hit the floor at Chamberlayne's feet. From somewhere outside he heard a strange whistling sound.

One of the worst times of all came on the following Monday. First, stones fell into the kitchen; then, while Chamberlayne was in his anteroom, another window there was broken by more stones. Naturally, all the neighbors were agog with curiosity and there were always some in and around the house in the daytime. Downstairs, where a group of them had gathered, twenty or thirty stones, some of them large, came out of an adjoining room and the curiosity seekers took to their heels for safety. All this time, now and then, there came the sound of three or four heavy blows, as if someone were wielding a sledge hammer.

Off and on during that week more rocks were thrown into the house. Outside, in the fields, Indian corn that had been planted was torn up by the roots and the field hands heard the eerie whistling again.

Something had to be done. No charges of witchcraft were made against the woman who had threatened Mr. Walton, presumably because the memory of the frightful injustice of the Salem witchcraft trials was too much on his mind, as well as the minds of those who would have to try her.

Nevertheless, the superstitious people of the region knew certain remedies against witches' spells, and the Waltons tried one of them. They put a pot filled with urine on the fire, threw in pins and boiled the liquid. This was supposed to be a sure way to deal out punishment to a witch or wizard who was making trouble. But a stone came flying through the air, knocked the pot off the fire, and broke its top, spilling the contents.

However, after that, the fall of the stones stopped. All through the month of August there were none. People began to think the charm against the evil spirit had broken its spell. But in September, when Mr. Walton started into town to attend a meeting of the governor's council, he was suddenly felled by three stones, each as large as his fist. One lacerated his head severely and the other two struck his back, injuring it so badly that he suffered pain in it to the day of his death.

The demon, spirit, witch or wizard seems to have been satisfied with this. Whether she was guilty or not, the woman who had predicted that Mr. Walton would never enjoy a foot of the land she had lost to him had had her revenge, since the pain he suffered could not have made his life very enjoyable.

What or who *did* cause the stoning? This is one witch story for which no reasonable explanation has ever been reached. The hot stones might have indicated a volcanic eruption except that New Hampshire's White Mountains are far from Portsmouth and none of them are volcanic, anyway. Another possible explanation might be showers of meteors from outer space, since such showers do sometimes strike the earth. But what of the bricks? Bricks do not bombard the earth from outer space, nor do erupting volcanoes spew them out. Besides, there were all the other queer happenings that such explanations cannot account for.

Did the incident of Lithobolia ever really happen? That George Chamberlayne wrote the story himself in 1698 in great detail cannot be doubted. If it were a tale he made up, he certainly had a fertile imagination. However, if it were false, he would scarcely have dared name the governor of Rhode Island and a former governor of West Jersey as eyewitnesses.

One other piece of information adds some credibility to the story. In January, 1652, the Portsmouth selectmen granted thirty feet of land along the shore of a cove on Great Island (today the island is Newcastle) to George Walton for the building of a storehouse. In September of that year they granted George Walton another acre "near unto his house." This may have been the same George Walton as a young man or perhaps his father, with the same name. And it does not seem impossible that one or the other of these grants may have caused the trouble with the old woman who threatened Mr. Walton for taking the land she believed was hers, although her curse came true a long time later.

Some force must have caused the stoning, if it did happen. Was it one which science has not yet discovered? After all, who would have believed, a hundred years ago, that people would sit in their living rooms and see other people moving about and speaking, hundreds, thousands of miles away, even as far as the moon, their images and words flashed instantly through the air by invisible electric waves? What will the twenty-first century bring in discoveries of things now unknown?

Or was the story of Lithobolia, the Stone-Throwing Demon in seventeenth-century New Hampshire, really witchcraft?

Another weird New Hampshire tale is that of the watching woman. Legend it may be, but as far as is known, no one has ever challenged the effort of the man who wrote it to tell what he honestly believed took place.

The Isles of Shoals, just off the New Hampshire coast, were a far better location for strange happenings in the first half of the nineteenth century than Portsmouth, for at that time they were lonely dots in the ocean inhabited only by a few fishermen and their families and not the popular summer resort that they later became.

There are eight islands, only about ten miles southeast

of Portsmouth. They are small—the largest, Appledore, is only 400 acres, while the next two in size are Star, 150 acres, and White, 55 acres. The rest are tiny islets, lonely and wild in those early days.

The weird story of the watching woman was told in great detail in a newspaper article published in the 1830s. For the sake of his health, the writer had gone to Star Island and remained there for some time, staying with the family of a fisherman.

One autumn morning he took a boat across to one of the other islands, intending to enjoy its solitude and a stroll along its rocky coast in the beautiful fall weather. The day was so calm that the sea was completely unruffled. The man climbed over the cliffs along the shore and onto a long, low point of land jutting out into the ocean toward the east. As he stood there looking out over the blue water, he suddenly realized that someone was standing near him, a woman swathed in a cloak, with her long blond hair flowing down over her shoulders. She said not a word, simply gazed into the distance.

The man decided she must be looking for a fishing boat returning with its catch and that some loved one would be aboard. He made bold to say to her, "Well, my pretty maiden, do you see anything of him?"

The girl turned and fixed her eyes on him. They were blue and held a look of deep sadness.

"He *will* come again," she replied, then walked away and disappeared behind a jutting rock.

There was nothing particularly strange about the incident, since a few people did live on the islet, yet something in the way the girl had spoken and the way she looked at him made the writer of the story intensely curious. He tried to convince himself that it had been a delusion caused by his illness, but he could not rest until he had gone back there again.

The next day the weather had changed. It was stormy, with the wind blowing a half gale, and the sick man's host, the fisherman, tried to dissuade him from setting out. Nevertheless, the writer was determined to go. He set the sail on his small boat and started out.

He was lucky that the wind and waves did not capsize his boat, and when he reached the coast of the islet near where he had seen the girl, the surf was so tumultuous that he could not possibly land. However, he steered the boat around to the leeward side of the island and was able to reach shore in the shelter of a small cove.

He then scrambled over the rocks and cliffs to the jutting point of land. This time, buffeted by the storm and drenched with spray from the crashing waves, he saw no one, but nevertheless he was sure that above the roar of the surf he heard a woman's voice: "He *will* come again," followed by low laughter.

From then on the man seemed to be enchanted. The lure of the strange woman drew him to the islet day after day, whenever the weather made it possible. Each time the watching young woman was there, and each time she repeated the same words. He noticed something else that made his blood run cold: her large blue eyes never moved when she looked at him but remained fixed with an unearthly stare.

Her gaze had such a strange effect on him that his illness grew worse. He wanted to stay away, but could not. At last, late one afternoon he sailed over to the islet and stood once more on the point. The girl appeared and stood beside him in the serenity of a beautiful sunset. It seemed to the writer that the scene had affected the mysterious girl, for when she fixed her eyes on him he thought he saw their icy coldness soften.

Then, as usual, she walked away and vanished. Several times before he had tried to follow her but always there was no trace, and he noticed that where she had trodden on shells along a sandy stretch of beach they had not been crushed.

Suddenly the man was overcome with terror. He knelt there on the shore and swore a solemn oath never to return again.

Back on Star Island, the fisherman in whose house the man was staying noticed his agitation. He told the writer he knew where he had been and what he had seen.

"I have seen her too," he said, and then he told the legend of the watching woman. When the Isles of Shoals were first settled in the seventeenth century, they were a favorite rendezvous for the pirates who then infested the seas. The most notorious one who came there was the infamous Captain Edward Teach, better known as Blackbeard.

Blackbeard's best-known operations were conducted from a base he established on the North Carolina coast, but like other pirates he roved the seas far and wide while he and his men seized and looted ships and killed their crews and passengers. It is not at all impossible that Blackbeard visited the Isles of Shoals or that he and other pirates buried treasure there. It is known that in the 1830s Captain Sam Haley found silver bars worth $3,000 there under a flat rock on little Smutty Nose Island.

The story that the writer's fisherman-host told was that

43

one of Blackbeard's comrades, a Captain Scot, had brought a beautiful girl to the Isles of Shoals; she may have been a passenger in one of the vessels that this buccaneer captured. Captain Scot had fallen in love with her and left her on the island, intending, no doubt, to return and retire on the booty he had amassed and hidden there.

Whether the girl fell in love with Captain Scot or whether he exercised some unearthly power over her, she is supposed to have sworn an oath to await his return after another voyage. But he never came back, possibly because, if the legend is true, the powder magazine of one of Blackbeard's ships blew up and destroyed the vessel. Captain Scot may have been one of the victims of the explosion. But the young woman remained on the island, ceaselessly watching for a sail on the horizon that would signal his return.

There is a sequel to the story which, if it is true, gives it an even more supernatural turn. One summer day a group of people came to the island for a day's pleasure. In the center of the island stood a deserted shanty built long before by fishermen and then abandoned.

While the members of the party were at their merry-making, the wind rose and one of them decided to go down to the shore and make sure the boats were all right. When he returned he was greatly agitated and knelt on the ground where the rest of the party were gathered.

"Do you know what I have seen?" he asked the others. "Coming back from the boats I found the fish house [the deserted shanty] and as I neared it I saw someone watching me from the window. Of course I thought it was one of you, but when I was near enough to recognize the face I perceived it to be the strange countenance of a woman, wan as death, a face young, yet with a look of infinite age. Old! It was older than the Sphinx in the desert. It looked as if it had been watching and waiting for me since the beginning of time. I walked straight into the hut. There wasn't a vestige of a human being there; it was absolutely empty."

The party hastily departed from the island. Was it the watching woman the visitor had seen? Where had she gone when he walked into the shanty? Was she alive or the ghost of the watching woman? What sort of magic could have preserved her like a living corpse, still waiting for her lover to return? Or had the investigator, perhaps recalling the story of the watching woman, imagined what he believed he had seen?

As for the man who wrote the newspaper story, did he imagine it or make it up? Was the illness that had sent him to the Isles of Shoals to recuperate a mental one? All are questions that cannot be answered, and this remains the unsolved mystery of the watching woman of the Isles of Shoals.

Another New England witchcraft legend in which some of the details seem to have a reasonable basis took place in Ipswich in the Massachusetts Bay colony. Ipswich is on the Massachusetts coast, north of Boston. Its very name suggests witchcraft; in fact, Elizabeth Howe of Ipswich was one of the executed victims of the Salem witchcraft delusion, and a number of the accused witches at that time were placed in the Ipswich jail because there was none in Salem Village.

One evil resident of Ipswich who gave its settlers good reason to suspect him of witchcraft after his death was Harry Main. No more wicked man ever lived there. He had been a pirate, a smuggler and a wrecker.

The trade of wrecking is an old one and was practiced in many parts of the world. A wrecker would place lights or bonfires near a seaport on a part of the shore where there were dangerous reefs or shoal water. The scheme was to decoy ships toward the land at night in the belief that the lights there were those of the seaport. When the ships were wrecked on the jagged reefs or grounded on a sand bar, the wreckers would go out in boats and loot the vessel of her cargo.

That Harry Main actually lived in Ipswich seems certain, since in the nineteenth century his house still stood in the town and was pointed out to visitors. His wrecking operations in the early days of the town were centered on Ipswich Bar, a sandy shoal along the coast there.

Harry Main was supposed to have amassed an immense fortune and buried it while he plied his wicked profession. When he died, every square foot in the garden of his home was dug up by hunters seeking the treasure, but never a piece of eight or a guinea was found.

A strange legend grew up about Harry Main: He was supposed to have sold his soul to the Devil. When it was claimed by Satan after Harry's death, he was said to have been chained to Ipswich Bar, where so many of his murderous activities had taken place. His doom was to remain there forever, trying to make a cable out of sand. When a gale rose and the great waves crashed over the bar, their roar was believed to be Harry Main's yells of rage as the surf smashed his cable of sand and he had to start all over. In Ipswich, mothers frightened balky children into obedience by threatening that Harry Main would get them if they did not behave.

Harry's treasure drew the attention of many an Ipswich resident. When his garden yielded nothing, they dug in other likely places, but with no result. At last an Ipswich man dreamed that the treasure was buried on a hill in the town. He put no faith in it until he had the same dream three nights in succession. He said nothing about it to anyone, however, knowing that the hill would surely be leveled immediately by treasure seekers. To get it all for himself, he waited until midnight on a dark night and set out for the hill, carrying a spade, a lantern and his Bible—the last no doubt to protect him from whatever he might encounter in the wake of this wicked man, perhaps even Satan himself in some guise, to prevent him from recovering the treasure.

The fortune hunter's dream had been so clear each time that he knew the exact spot to begin his digging. Driven by his lust for money and fear of the unknown, the man dug with desperate energy. His heart bounded when the spade struck a hard object. Down in the hole, he managed to scrape the dirt away from a flat stone with a bar of iron across it. He pried the bar loose and held it in his hand as he prepared to lift the stone.

At that moment he was suddenly surrounded by a host of cats whose eyeballs gleamed eerily in the light of the lantern. He was petrified with fear, but was able to lift his spade and cry, "Scat!"

The cats vanished and the treasure seeker found himself up to his waist in cold water which had somehow gushed into the hole. He scrambled out, the iron bar still clutched in his trembling hand, and sloshed down the hill to his home.

He still had the iron bar as a souvenir of his hair-raising adventure. He had it made into a door latch by the local blacksmith. For years it was shown to Ipswich visitors as proof of the legend of Harry Main's treasure. Perhaps even today, if his house still stands among the ancient ones of Ipswich and could be located, the relic might be seen.

As for Harry Main's gold, the treasure hunter did no more seeking; he had had enough of it. So Harry's ill-gotten fortune, if he did bury it somewhere in or around Ipswich, still remains for the digging if someone can locate the spot and dares defy some of Satan's favorite familiars—cats.

HECHERY IN PENNSYLVANIA

The lovely, rolling farmlands of eastern Pennsylvania, west of Philadelphia, have become one of the great tourist attractions of the United States. In summer the highways are choked with vacationing Americans who want to see the "Pennsylvania Dutch country." Among the principal attractions are the Mennonites and their close religious relatives, the Amish. Since these people shun the use of modern contrivances such as the telephone, radio, television and automobile, visitors get a thrill out of seeing old-fashioned, horse-drawn buggies, well closed in, clip-clopping along the roads of the region. It takes a good photographer to get a closeup picture of these vehicles, since the Mennonites and Amish are averse to cameras and will use every possible means to avoid having their pictures taken.

Another lure is the food. Restaurants in the Pennsylvania Dutch country serve some of the finest home-cooked meals to be found anywhere—hearty German-style cuisine which uses mostly home-produced ingredients.

However, a third attraction that draws thousands to the

Pennsylvania Dutch country is its reputation for witchcraft, kept in the public mind by the region's famous "hex marks." One sees these fantastic symbols on the enormous barns that usually dwarf the adjacent farmhouses of their owners. And now that the tourist trade rivals farming as a source of revenue in the Pennsylvania Dutch country, one may buy replicas of hex marks in any gift shop along the main highways.

What is a hex mark? It was used in Pennsylvania for years, and sometimes still is, as a protection against witches and their evil arts. Most of the marks use the star as a basic design, with five, six, eight and sometimes more points, usually enclosed in a circle. The circle is ordinarily white, but the stars may be black, yellow, sky blue and other colors.

To understand how hex marks came to the Pennsylvania Dutch country, it is necessary to go far back into history. There are several theories as to how hex marks originated. One, quite well supported by evidence, is that these symbols originated in a Cult of the Sun during the Bronze Age, which lasted from about 2000 to 1800 B.C. in Europe, when the people discovered that copper and tin could be melted and mixed or alloyed to form a strong metal that was far better than stone for making such implements as swords, awls, knives, hammers and arms.

The Sun Cult flourished throughout Europe in the Bronze Age, and many archaeologists and ethnologists think the hex marks were originated by this cult. At least one notable authority, however, believes that they were brought to Europe from the Mediterranean in ships from Crete and Mycenae in Asia Minor. And the swastikas with the curved, club-shaped arms often used in hex marks probably had their origin in India in prehistoric times and gradually spread east and west from there.

As for the Pennsylvania Dutch hex marks, they were brought from Germany and the German-speaking part of Switzerland in the seventeenth and eighteenth centuries. This queer import came to America largely as a result of William Penn's efforts to settle and enlarge his American colony of Pennsylvania.

Penn may be called the first of the great American land promoters. He came to America in 1682 and founded Philadelphia, hoping that it would live up to the meaning of its name—the City of Brotherly Love. Like Rhode Island, Pennsylvania was established as a colony where there would be complete religious freedom.

Penn stayed only long enough to get Philadelphia well started, draw up laws for the new colony and make a lasting treaty of friendship with the Indians of the region. Then, leaving Pennsylvania in the hands of able associates, he returned to England. His object was to publicize the new colony as the finest place in the world to live, work and prosper. To accomplish this he had pamphlets printed in several languages, describing Pennsylvania's beauty and the opportunity it offered to new settlers. These pamphlets were widely distributed in England, Wales, Scotland, Ireland, Germany and Switzerland.

They had a special appeal to the people of that part of Germany called the Lower Palatinate, including the Rhineland, and also to German-speaking Switzerland. For many years before that, Europe had been torn by continual wars in which armies marched into these regions, looting, despoiling, killing and terrorizing the people. Once the wars ended, these regions were ruled by petty princes, many of them tyrants who imposed backbreaking taxes on the common people in order that they themselves might live in luxury.

The people of these areas of Germany and Switzerland were ripe for a change to relieve the poverty and misery of their lives. They flocked to Pennsylvania by the thousands, enduring great hardships and miserable conditions during the journey, but come they did, along with many English, Irish, Scots and other Europeans who were dissatisfied with conditions in their countries. But it was largely the Germans and Swiss who settled in the fertile farmlands west of Philadelphia.

"Pennsylvania Dutch" does not properly describe these people. Since they spoke German, and the word for "German" in their language is "*Deutsch*" (pronounced "Doytch"), English-speaking settlers corrupted it to "Dutch." The Pennsylvania Dutch should actually be called Pennsylvania *Deutsch*—Pennsylvania Germans.

With them, the German-speaking settlers brought the hex marks they had used for centuries in Germany and Switzerland. In these countries, during the sixteenth and seventeenth centuries, thousands of accused witches were executed in horrible fashion, for practically everyone believed that witches did exist. The convicted witches usually died by burning at the stake, due to the religious zeal against witchcraft on the part of both Protestants and Catholics. What happened there made the twenty executions of the Salem witchcraft delusion in Massachusetts in 1692 look like a pink-tea party.

Superstitions about witchcraft made the people turn to what they believed were magical protections against the evil designs of witches. In Germany and Switzerland, hex marks were a favorite means of driving witches away. And the German-speaking immigrants, when they arrived in Pennsylvania, saw no reason why the Devil, through witches,

52

should not be at work in America too, and they used the hex marks in their new homeland to protect themselves and their property.

The reason the tourist in the Pennsylvania Dutch country sees the hex marks on barns is because the upper story of the early barns was made of wood, where hex marks could easily be painted; they could not so readily be put on the lower story, which was made of stone, nor could they be put on the houses, which were generally also of stone. Nevertheless, in the old days, the Pennsylvania Dutch often put hex marks on their household utensils too.

For years, in German-speaking parts of Europe, hex marks had been charms to keep witches away. Placed on a barn, they were supposed to protect the farm's precious livestock and also to keep the barn from being struck by lightning, which was believed to be one of Satan's black arts.

The Mennonites, especially the Amish branch, whose interpretations of the Bible's commands as to how they should live are even stricter, avoid using hex marks—which are considered sinful. In fact, the Pennsylvania Dutch who do use them are sensitive about it and are apt to tell visitors that the marks are simply decorations.

Nevertheless, there is little doubt that hex marks were used in the past as a defense against witches. One authority says that the original hex marks had an opening on the outside. The idea was that the witch, trying to get into a barn through the opening, would become entangled in the hex design and, unable to find her way out, would be trapped there, helpless to do harm to cattle or to torment the people in the farmhouse. This writer tells of seeing one of these ancient devices, called a *drudenfusz* (sometimes a *hexenfusz*) or witch's foot. It was carved in a circular design into the lintel or headpiece inside a barn door and had an opening on the outside.

Some Pennsylvania Dutch feared witches so much that they did not depend entirely upon hex marks to protect them. Certain objects believed to have power against witchcraft were shoved under the doorsill of the cow stable, mystic symbols were chalked on door posts and herbs supposed to repel witches were hung near the cattle stalls to keep the cows from giving bloody milk or from drying up and giving none—both conditions believed to be the work of witches. As for the horses, a "hag stone" ("hag," though generally used to describe an ugly old woman, can also mean a witch), a stone with a hole in it, would be tied to the door latch of the horse stable. A horseshoe nailed over a door is supposed to bring good luck, and many an old American house has one or more. Pennsylvania was one of the regions where the horseshoe was believed to be a protection against witches.

Hex is the German word for witch and *hexerei* for witchcraft. These terms, in Pennsylvania, became corrupted to "hech" and "hechery." A person who was "heched" was bewitched. Belief in hechery was not confined to the Pennsylvania Dutch in that colony. The many settlers from England, Scotland and Wales brought with them their own beliefs in witchcraft and superstitions about it.

One object the Pennsylvania settlers believed was used by witches was the Black Book. The Black Book was supposed to contain the sixth and seventh books of Moses and to be a dictionary of the black art of witchcraft. This is one of the legends that grew up about Moses after his death. That he wrote the Pentateuch, the first five books of the Old Testament, is not disputed by either Christians or Jews. In them are set down the story of God's creation of the world, the wanderings and sufferings of the Israelites and the laws given Moses by God which the people of the earth are directed to obey. But one of the legends about Moses has it that he learned witchcraft while the Israelites were in bondage in Egypt and put this knowledge in his sixth and seventh books, called the Black Book, which is bound in black leather and printed on black parchment. This is without doubt simply a legend and untrue. But in Pennsylvania many people did believe in the existence of the Black Book. Ownership of a copy was grounds for suspicion that the person who had it was a witch.

In an early Pennsylvania settlement called Pine Station, an old woman, Granny McGill, was believed to have had a copy of the Black Book. When a family in the village began to have serious trouble, they immediately suspected Granny McGill.

The story goes that the cows belonging to the family, the Quigleys, began to give bloody milk. Knowing what to do, they put some of the bloody milk in a pan and heated it until it became a solid mass. Into this, using a silver knife, the sign of the cross was carved while they repeated the words of a charm against witchcraft.

A few days later the Quigleys had a visitor—Granny McGill, moaning that she had spilled some hot lard and burned her hand. The Quigleys applied a remedy for a burn to Granny's hand, and after that there was no more blood in the milk. So goes one of the many Pennsylvania witchcraft legends. If it did happen, it was a most incredible coincidence—unless one prefers to believe it really was witchcraft.

The Quigleys took credit for exposing another suspected

witch, Granny Jung. One day when Granny Jung was seen at a distance coming toward the Quigley farm, Mrs. Quigley put a new broom under the front doorstep. "If Granny Jung is a witch she will never be able to walk over that broomstick," she said.

Granny Jung was indeed coming to call at the Quigley house. As she came toward the door she reached down and pulled out the hidden broom by the handle. "Why, here's a brand new besom [an old word for broom]," she said. "I wonder what it is doing here." Thus the Quigleys were sure that Granny Jung was a real witch, according to the legend.

Suspected witches in the Quigleys' neighborhood seem to have sought the family's aid often when in trouble. Granny Crispin, a neighbor named George Wilson and a mysterious wolf were also involved in another tale about them.

Late one afternoon, Wilson saw a huge wolf skulking along the edge of a field. He raised his musket, fired and saw he had hit the animal in the left foreleg. It fell down, but before Wilson could reload, it got up and staggered off into the woods.

Soon afterward, Granny Crispin came to the Quigley house in great pain. Her left arm was broken. "Oh, help me!" she cried. "I slipped on the goosegrass in the yard and the brittle old bone in my arm snapped like a pipestem." The Quigleys put a splint on Granny Crispin's arm, and the giant wolf was seen no more.

It is not strange that some of the Pennsylvania witchcraft beliefs were strikingly similar to those in some of the other American colonies. These regions all had settlers from Britain who brought their own beliefs with them.

For example, in Pennsylvania as elsewhere, if knots were

found in a horse's mane and tail in the morning and the animal was sweating, it meant that a witch had put the knots there to assist her in mounting and riding the horse all night at great speed, performing her evil deeds throughout the countryside. In Pennsylvania they braided the horse's mane and tail with corn husks, making it impossible for a witch to mount her steed.

Sometimes, when a housewife was churning, no butter would form. To make the butter come, a silver coin was dropped into the churn to break the spell a witch had put on it. This was also done in New England and some other colonies. In Pennsylvania another method was sometimes used: chips would be filed off a horseshoe, heated red-hot and dropped into the churn. This was supposed to drive off the witch and her evil spell by causing bits of sizzling metal to run into her hand.

Following this custom, according to Pennsylvania witchcraft lore, a young girl in Clinton County was dropping the hot metal into the churn when a notorious supposed witch, Granny Myers, suddenly appeared and struck the girl a smart blow on the hip, saying, "I put a spell on you!" That night, when the young woman went to bed she discovered the mark of a horseshoe where the witch had struck her. The brand was very painful and took several months to heal, and the horseshoe mark remained there for the rest of the girl's life. This is another witch tale that one may believe or not.

The sign of the cross was used by housewives baking bread. If the dough did not rise, it was considered the work of a witch, but this could be prevented by marking the dough with a cross before it went into the oven. When a spinning wheel would not work, the hechery could be defeated by tying a sprig of mountain ash to a spoke of the wheel. And people who met a suspected witch on a road were careful to pass her on the right to avoid trouble.

The use of silver bullets to kill a witch was common in Pennsylvania as well as in other colonies. It was not unusual for muskets used in colonial days to misfire or "flash in the pan." In damp weather this was even more common, but deer and bear hunters who had such troubles blamed them on a witch. Or perhaps their dogs would refuse to chase a quarry, especially if it were a bear they had learned to fear. This too was blamed on witchcraft.

If a certain supposed witch was suspected, the hunters would draw a picture of her and fire a silver bullet into it. It was claimed that the suspected witch would sometimes die soon afterward. Since most of them were old women, the death of one might well have seemed to be due to the silver bullet. Another way of disabling a witch was to get a hair from her head, wrap it in a piece of paper, place the package against a tree and fire a silver bullet into it.

Like many other early Americans, Pennsylvania settlers used charms to protect themselves against witchcraft. One charm was a small linen or canvas bag pinned to a person's outer garment or worn around the neck on a string. On the bag, hand-printed in red ink, were the letters INRI, the initials of the Latin phrase placed over Jesus' head on the cross: "Jesus of Nazareth, King of the Jews." Below each letter was the sign of the cross. Inside the bag a piece of paper was inscribed with the "blessings and forbiddings" said to be in the seventh book of Moses. These were written in German, with every other line spelled out backwards. The words were religious, forbidding any witch to come anywhere near the person wearing the charm. This charm is another illustration of the close relationship of witchcraft to religion.

A certain amount of religion and the healing type of witchcraft are combined in an old Pennsylvania Dutch practice called "powwow." As everyone knows, "powwow" is an Indian word describing a discussion or conference. How it got into the language of the Pennsylvania settlers is something of a mystery, but it might have been borrowed from the red men and transferred into a different meaning.

Powwow healers could be either men or women. To cure an ailing patient they used a combination of a charm or incantation—usually religious—along with the familiar witchcraft remedies made from herbs, roots, leaves and sometimes other very odd materials. To impress the patient with his magical powers, the powwow healer would mutter meaningless incantations, make strange movements with his hands and use charms. Powwow healers were little different from Indian medicine men or the so-called white witches who do only good. With all of them the real power lay in their knowledge of herbal remedies and the ability to give the patient confidence that he was getting better. Powwow healers were highly regarded in Pennsylvania.

In addition to the powwow healers, the Pennsylvania Dutch had their own remedies for common ailments. To cure a toothache it was only necessary to stab the tooth with a nail until it bled, and then to put a mixture of vinegar and meal in a piece of cloth wrapped around a piece of apple tree root and bury it. It would seem that some people might have preferred to let the tooth ache.

To cure bleeding, one counted backwards from fifty to

three. For snake bites a charm could be recited: "God has created all things, and they were good. Thou only, serpent, are damned. Cursed be thou and thy sting. Zing. Zing. Zing." It would be interesting to know how many people survived Pennsylvania rattlesnake or copperhead bites by the use of this unusual formula.

Prevention of accidents was easy. All one had to do was sew to his right sleeve the eye of a wolf. As for warts, simply stick a pin through the wart and give the pin away. The warts would follow the pin. Again, to quote an ancient maxim: "There are some remedies worse than the disease."

Although Pennsylvania was founded on a basis of complete religious freedom, it did have a few trials concerned with witchcraft, several as late as the twentieth century. The earliest was in 1683, a year after Pennsylvania was established. Two Swedish women, Margaret Mattson and Yeshro Hendrickson, were accused as witches. William Penn was still in Pennsylvania and presided at the trial.

Yeshro Hendrickson appears to have pleaded guilty, but Margaret Mattson claimed she was innocent. Witnesses against her told stories, without any real evidence, of how she had bewitched animals and poultry. For some reason oxen were said to be immune from her spells. As happened in at least one witchcraft trial in Massachusetts, Margaret Mattson's own daughter is said to have stated that her mother was a witch. But Pennsylvanians were not like the ruthless Puritan witch hunters of Massachusetts, and Margaret Mattson was found guilty "of having the common fame of a witch, but not guilty of the manner or form of which she stands indicted." Both women were allowed to post bail as security for their future good behavior and were released.

Pennsylvania, from its earliest beginnings, was a place

where belief in witchcraft was rampant, yet it had no terrible executions like those in Massachusetts. Perhaps this was because the settlers, especially the Germans and English, had heard too much of or in some cases seen the frightful witch hunts, tortures and executions by burning in their countries during the sixteenth and seventeenth centuries.

✿ ✿ ✿ 5
THE DEVIL IN MARYLAND
AND VIRGINIA

Witchcraft and witchcraft trials flourished in the colonies immediately south of Pennsylvania, but there were only a scattering of convictions and even fewer executions than took place in New England in the seventeenth century.

In the mountainous western part of Maryland, beliefs in ghosts and "hants" were stronger than that in witches, though there are plenty of witch legends there, too. In the more heavily populated areas in the east there were some witchcraft trials, but only one hanging for witchcraft is recorded.

Curiously, in one early witchcraft case with which Maryland was concerned, neither the supposed witchcraft nor its punishment by hanging took place in Maryland, but aboard the ship *Charity of London,* bound from England to Maryland in 1654. In the old days sailors were a notoriously superstitious lot. Ships would not sail on a Friday, an unlucky day. Masters of outgoing vessels often had a horoscope cast by an astrologer showing the exact day, hour and minute the ship should sail for a safe and prosperous voyage. Even in modern times, whistling aboard ships of the United States Navy has been discouraged, a superstition of bad luck that has been carried on more or less out of tradition.

When, during a stormy voyage, the *Charity of London* developed a leak that grew worse daily, the crew became suspicious that a passenger, Mary Lee, had bewitched the vessel. They went to Captain John Bosworth about it. He was not disposed to take action without some evidence and he asked the sailors why they thought the woman was a witch. They replied that they knew it from her speech and actions, and demanded that she be tried immediately.

Although this evidence did not convince the vessel's master, he decided to put the accused woman ashore in Bermuda, which was not too far away. However, due to the continued bad weather, cross winds prevented him from landing there.

Captain Bosworth then consulted with the ship's mate, a Mr. Chipsham. They decided that in order to avoid possible trouble with the hands, they must try Mary Lee. Since two or three other ships were in sight at the time, Bosworth wanted to bring their masters aboard to help pass judgment, but the mountainous seas made it impossible for small boats to bring the other captains aboard.

The seamen then took matters into their own hands. They seized Mary Lee, searched her, found what they considered to be a witch mark and called Captain Bosworth and Mr. Chipsham to see it. Then they lashed the woman to the anchor capstan and left her there overnight.

The records are scanty, but it appears that in the morning Mary Lee confessed that she was a witch. Possibly she may have considered herself to be one or perhaps confessed in fear of torture. It is far more likely that the leak in the ship

was caused by the storm than by witchcraft, but nevertheless, the sailors then visited Captain Bosworth in his cabin
and demanded that Mary Lee be put to death.

The master did not want to do so, but probably fearing a
mutiny he might not be able to handle, he emulated Pontius
Pilate in the New Testament of the Bible when the fate of
Jesus was put up to the Roman governor; the captain washed
his hands of the whole affair and told the seamen to do as
they pleased with the accused witch. Mary Lee was then
hanged from the yardarm.

The *Charity of London* arrived safely at St. Mary's in
Maryland. Although the case was considered within the juris-
diction of the colony, since the vessel was bound there, no
action appears to have been taken against the crew. There
was a good reason for this.

Maryland had been founded in 1634 by Lord Baltimore as
a refuge for Catholics, who were persecuted in other American colonies. But since the colony was established as one
with full freedom of religion, in 1649 a group of Puritans who
had been banished from Virginia founded Providence, today
Annapolis, the capital of Maryland. By 1654, when the *Charity of London* incident took place, the Puritans had increased
in numbers and strength. After King Charles I of England
was beheaded in 1649 and the Puritans there took control of
the government with Oliver Cromwell as Protector in place
of a king, the Maryland Puritans seized control of the entire
Maryland colony.

Being Puritans, who favored ruthless hunting down and
extermination of witches, the Maryland authorities were
evidently not disposed to punish anyone for Mary Lee's execution. Two of the *Charity of London*'s passengers did appear for questioning before Governor William Stone, as well

as before the colony's secretary and a member of the Maryland Council, but there the matter seems to have ended.

Four years later there was another, similar case with the same result. In 1658, while a vessel named the *Sarah Artch* was bound from England to Maryland, an accused passenger, Elizabeth Richardson, was hanged at sea as a witch. The affair came to light when none other than John Washington of Virginia, great-grandfather of George Washington, charged Edward Prescott, a merchant who owned the *Sarah Artch* and was aboard during the voyage, with the crime. How Mr. Washington learned of it and why he acted is not known.

This time the accused merchant-shipowner was arrested and tried for murder. Prescott did not deny that Elizabeth Richardson had been hanged by the vessel's master and the ship's company, but said that the crew were ready to mutiny if the supposed witch were not destroyed. No witnesses appeared against Prescott and he was acquitted, another probable example of the Maryland Puritan government's witch-hunting zeal.

Later, even though the Puritan government in England had fallen and with it that of Maryland, there were several witchcraft trials in the colony, but only one execution.

In 1665 Elizabeth Bennett was accused of witchcraft. The case was brought before a grand jury at St. Mary's, but she never came to trial since she was cleared of the charge.

In 1674 John Cowman was not so lucky, though he managed to escape hanging. He was accused of bewitching Elizabeth Goodale, tried and sentenced to be executed. But enough members of the lower house of the Maryland Assembly were skeptical of witchcraft to appeal to Governor Charles Calvert to save Cowman. The governor reprieved him, but ordered him taken to the gallows, where the hangman's noose was to be put around his neck. Then he was to be employed at whatever work the governor wished for as long as Calvert decided the punishment should last.

Rebecca Fowler had no luck at all, however. She was indicted as a witch, tried before the colony's attorney general and a panel of jurors, found guilty and hanged on October 9, 1685.

A number of other witchcraft cases were tried in Maryland in the latter part of the seventeenth century, but all the accused witches were found not guilty. Thus Maryland had only one witchcraft execution within the colony itself to blot its record in that respect.

In western Maryland there were "witches" galore, but the people there, not only in the early days but in more modern ones, had their ways of protecting themselves against witchcraft, although many of their legends and folklore stories tell of witches who succeeded in their deviltry.

Some of these stories have an odd resemblance to witchcraft tales in other parts of America. One is about a farmer who had a valuable horse he thought was bewitched. In the area lived an old man named Stokes, who had a reputation for ridding people of witchcraft spells. The farmer promised Stokes fifty dollars if he would lift the enchantment from the horse. The old man took a hoop off a barrel and passed it over the horse's head, meanwhile muttering words that no one could understand. When he replaced the hoop on the barrel, he asked the farmer if he should hammer it down hard. "Go ahead," was the reply. "I don't care if you kill the witch."

While the old man was vigorously plying the hammer, the farmer's little boy came running out of the house. "If you don't stop," he shouted at Stokes, "my mother says you'll kill her."

Witch or no witch, the farmer loved his wife so devotedly that he became angry at the old man for hurting his wife and refused to pay the fifty dollars. The legend does not say whether the horse recovered or whether old Stokes ever got his money. But it is among several tales in which one of a married couple did not know that the other was a witch.

In western Maryland broomsticks and salt appear, as they do in other early American witchcraft lore, as protection against witches. One tale concerns a woman whose reputation as a witch was well established in the settlement where she lived. One day she came to call on a neighbor and stayed so long that the people began to wonder, especially since the suspected witch had left someone who was ill alone in her house. It was nearly nightfall before it was discovered that a broomstick had fallen across the doorway. When it was removed, the caller took to her heels and scooted home as fast as she could.

The next day the supposed witch came to call again. This time, when the family saw her coming, they put salt under the chair in which they seated their visitor. Again the woman sat and sat, apparently anchored there, until the salt was removed, when she left again with all speed. Now firmly convinced that she was a witch, the people in the house drove nails into her tracks in the soil. After seeing nothing of her for several days, the family learned she was laid up in her cabin with sore feet. They finally took pity on her and removed the nails from her footprints, and the witch's sore feet soon healed.

As in other parts of the country, the use of a silver bullet to destroy a witch crops up in Maryland, presumably after photography came into use in the nineteenth century. According to one version, the witch's victim would get a photograph of her if possible; otherwise, her profile would be drawn on the wall of a barn. The silver bullet would then be fired into the witch's image. There was also a belief in Maryland that in order to make animals, usually livestock, fall ill, a witch would fire her own bullets, made of pith or hair, into their bodies.

The widely accepted belief that witches could fly by anointing themselves with a magic oil, grease or ointment was also common in Maryland. A story about this concerns a Black family, a girl, her mother and her grandmother, in the western Maryland mountains.

The grandmother, known in the community as Aunt Sarah, smoked an ancient pipe of which she was very fond. She said it had been handed down to her mother and then to herself from her grandmother, who had been a witch. Often Aunt Sarah would wake in the night and want her pipe, so it was the granddaughter's duty to fill the pipe with tobacco before going to bed, and also to get up in the night and light the pipe when her grandmother called for it.

However, quite often Aunt Sarah would tell the girl not to bother, since she would not want the pipe that night. Accustomed to being called, the girl would frequently arouse anyway. Each time, she found she was alone in the cabin, both her mother and grandmother missing.

Her curiosity became so great that one night when Aunt Sarah said she would not want her pipe, the girl pretended to be asleep, but peeped out from under the covers. She saw her grandmother and mother rubbing their bodies with rabbit fat. Then, three times, they repeated: "Up and out and away we go!" The third time they both flew up the chimney.

The girl got up, rubbed herself with rabbit fat and three times chanted, "Up and about and away we go!" Away she did go, but not up the chimney. All night, until dawn, she went flying around the room, bumping into walls and rafters.

The next night the grandmother and mother flew up the chimney again after the granddaughter had watched and listened as before. Suddenly the girl realized she had used the word "about" in her chant instead of "out." She tried again, saying "out" and this time she flew up the chimney. Outside, she saw her grandmother and mother mounting horses which carried them away into the darkness at break-neck speed. One horse, a yearling, was left; the girl mounted it and sped through the countryside, returning near dawn, just ahead of the other two women.

So goes the Maryland legend, and if it is believed, one may wonder whether the granddaughter, in time, also became a witch.

In neighboring Virginia there are no persecutions or witchcraft trials recorded for nearly twenty years after the first permanent settlement at Jamestown in 1607. Nevertheless, the early Virginians believed they lived in the midst of a rabble of devils who were among the forces of Satan—the Algonquian tribes of Indians who inhabited Virginia. Everything about them—their chiefs, their priests or medicine men and their ceremonies—smacked of the worst kind of witchcraft. These early settlers were sure that the Virginia Indians' god, Okaee (sometimes spelled Okee) was actually the Devil himself.

Even though the famous Captain John Smith, by becoming friendly enough with the Indians to trade with them for food, was largely responsible for the colony's survival during its first winter, he spoke of the red men time after time as devils. He said that the equally famous Chief Powhatan was "more like a devil then a man, with some two hundred as blacke [evil] as himselfe." Of course, Smith had reason to consider Powhatan a satanic man, since the Virginia leader would have been clubbed to death by Powhatan's order save for what is accepted as truth by many historians—the intervention of Pocahontas.

As time went on, other "great witches," as the colonists called the Indians, appeared in Virginia, but they were white, not red. With settlement spreading and the population increasing, witchcraft accusations and trials of settlers themselves occurred. However, as in most of the original colonies, there was no real torture and little persecution. This seems to be due partly to the attitude of the clergy, who were mainly Anglican and opposed harsh punishment of accused witches, and partly because Puritan settlement in Virginia was not encouraged or even tolerated to any extent.

However, there were a number of witchcraft cases. The first one, although it was sensational, was never actually tried, although a great deal of evidence was heard by the Virginia General Court, acting as a grand jury with Governor George Yeardley presiding. It took place in September, 1626, when neighbors of Goodwife Jane Wright, who lived across the James River from Jamestown, presented testimony, probably malicious and mostly absurd.

The evidence of the first witness was partly what is known as "hearsay," which is not accepted today by any court in the United States without further proof. A militia lieutenant from the fort across the river testified that he had heard a sergeant say he was "crossed" by a woman for a whole year, during which he could hit nothing he shot at. He added that the sergeant claimed that since Goodwife Wright was a midwife, she was angry because the sergeant's wife had used another midwife to attend her when their child was born. Moreover, said the lieutenant, he himself had fallen ill for three weeks, and after a child was born to his wife it was sick for two months; it recovered for a month and then for five weeks was in terrible pain.

Either Goodwife Wright was an extremely disagreeable woman who made many enemies or she had a number of spiteful neighbors. One, Rebecca Greye, testified that her husband's death had been correctly prophesied by Goodwife Wright, as well as the deaths of two men's wives. Rebecca was followed by other witnesses who gave similar testimony about Goodwife Wright's talent in foretelling doom.

A plantation owner's wife then came forward with an incriminating story that also appears to have been hearsay. Some wood had been stolen and a servant girl was suspected. Goodwife Wright had told the girl that if the stolen property was not returned she would make the servant dance naked, and lo! the next morning the stolen wood was back in its place.

Another witness referred to Goodwife Wright's reputation in England before she had come to America. There, said the witness, it was well known that Goodwife Wright was a witch.

The accused woman had only one friend at the investigation—her husband. Goodman Wright testified that in all the sixteen years of their marriage he had never seen or heard anything that made him suspect that his wife was a witch.

In Salem, Massachusetts, in 1692, such testimony would promptly have sent Goodwife Wright to the gallows. But Governor Yeardley and the members of the Virginia General

71

Court were no Puritan witch hunters. There is no record that the case ever came to trial.

For fifteen years after that no witchcraft trial in Virginia is recorded. In 1641 one was held when Jane Rookens accused George Barker's wife of being a witch. This one backfired against Jane Rookens, since the evidence indicated that she was a common scandalmonger. When she took the stand as a witness, she said she could not remember what had happened and that she was sorry. Her husband was ordered to pay the Barkers' expenses for the trial, as well as the court costs.

One man, William Harding of Northumberland County, accused of witchcraft and sorcery by a minister, was convicted by a jury of twenty-four men, but he was not hanged. He was sentenced to ten stripes on his back at the whipping post and banishment from Virginia.

Virginia had a witchcraft case similar to the one in Maryland that took place aboard the *Charity of London*, since it also involved a ship at sea bound for Jamestown in 1654. The records are scanty and do not even mention the name of the ship, but simply that "Capt Bennett had to appear at the Admiralty Court to answer to putting to death of Kath Grady as a witch at sea." Probably it was much like the *Charity of London* case, with either damage to the vessel in a storm or an epidemic of illness being blamed on Katherine Grady by the superstitious crew. However, in the Virginia case, for some reason Captain Bennett appears to have supervised the hanging of the accused witch. Yet the records show no action having been taken against Bennett by the court.

One curious twist in the history of Virginia's witchcraft troubles was that as accusations increased, instead of their causing a witchcraft delusion like that of Massachusetts, they made jurors in the colony sick and tired of hearing cases in which trivial and ridiculous evidence was given against accused witches. As a result, the courts turned on witnesses who gave malicious or trifling testimony and began to punish them. In 1655 in Linhaven (today Lynnhaven) it was ordered that anyone making accusations which could not be proved should be fined 1,000 pounds of tobacco. (Tobacco, Virginia's principal and most valuable crop, was often used like money in colonial days.)

Then, in 1659, a notorious gossip, Ann Godby, was brought into court on the charge of "Slander & scandalls Cast uppon Women under the notion of Witches." One of the victims of Goodwife Godby's malicious tongue, a Mistress Robinson, was named in the charges as having her good name abused. The court ordered Ann Godby's husband fined 300 pounds of tobacco in a hogshead, to pay all the court costs, and also £20 a day to the witnesses who had appeared, for their trouble.

So many husbands had to pay damages for their wives' clacking tongues that in 1662 the Virginia General Court took pity on them. It passed a law providing that a wife convicted of slander should be punished by ducking. The ducking stool was a well-known form of punishment for women adjudged to be common scolds in colonial times. A chair was fastened to one end of a long pole that was pivoted, seesaw-like, through a hole in an upright post. This apparatus stood by a millpond; the gossip or scold was tied into the chair and lowered into the water. The punishment was public, adding shame as well as discomfort to the woman in the ducking stool.

In colonial times many disputes over land boundaries

were taken to court. One such suit in Virginia involved quarrelsome Captain William Carver, a man of consequence in Lower Norfolk County, being a justice of the peace and a former member of Virginia's governing body, the House of Burgesses. His high standing did him no good, however, for the court decided the boundary suit in favor of his opponents, Lazarus and Jane Jenkins.

Vengeful Captain Carver then charged Jane Jenkins with being "familiar with evil spiritts and using witchcraft, &c." Jane might have been in serious trouble if any evidence had been found against her. The authorities tried; they searched her for witch marks and her house for the well-known images used to work evil spells. Apparently nothing was found, for Jane Jenkins was not brought to trial and Captain Carver was left to sulk over his lost land.

Other witchcraft cases in Virginia came to nothing until 1706, when the colony's most famous witchcraft trial took place. James and Grace Sherwood lived in Princess Anne County (originally Lower Norfolk). Grace was evidently highly unpopular with her neighbors. But when, in 1698, John and Jane Gisburne charged that Grace Sherwood was a witch who had put a spell on their cotton and bewitched their pigs to death, the Sherwoods sued them, Richard Capps and Elizabeth Barnes for slander.

In court, Elizabeth Barnes said that Grace Sherwood had appeared to her one night, and then left, through either the keyhole or cracks in the door, "like a black Catt." This often-used witchcraft charge was not believed by the jury, although the record does not show whether the Sherwoods obtained damages.

After that, Grace Sherwood appears to have continued

to be hated and suspected by her neighbors. In 1706 they tried to bring her to trial as a witch, but the court was skeptical of their charges. Finally, however, a jury composed of justices of the peace was convened, and ordered Grace "by her own Consent to be tried in the water by Ducking."

In this instance, "Ducking" meant an old custom used in England and sometimes in America of "swimming a witch." At the time when the infamous "Witch-Finder Generall," Matthew Hopkins, was operating in England, he considered this test one of the best for detecting a witch. The wretched woman was bound and thrown into a stream or pond. If she floated it meant that the water would have none of her and therefore she was a witch. If she sank she was innocent. A rope was tied to her to haul her out, but sometimes when the woman sank, thus proving her innocence, she drowned before they could remove her.

On July 10, Grace Sherwood was taken to a nearby plantation with her arms and legs bound and put into the millpond. She floated; but to make doubly sure she was a witch, they searched her and found two so-called witch marks on her body. All this evidence was enough to hang her, as it surely would have in Massachusetts at the time of the witchcraft delusion. She was imprisoned in the "Common Gaol" in irons to await trial. But there is no further account of the case and it appears that again Virginia justice was tempered with mercy, for there is a record of a will of a Grace Sherwood, dated in 1733.

As for the Black slaves in Maryland and Virginia, nothing seems to be known of their witchcraft practices, although they undoubtedly brought their own forms of it, including voodoo and obeah, from Africa. But apparently in both colonies they kept it a well-guarded secret—and with good reason—so that the "white folks" would not know what they were doing.

Going westward, into the mountains once more, witch-craft beliefs flourished in West Virginia, which was a part of Virginia until the Civil War, when some of the western counties disagreed with Virginia's decision to secede from the Union, joined with the Union and became the state of West Virginia in 1863.

The early settlers of this region were typically supersti-tious mountaineers and their witch tales reflect it. The stories are curiously like the legends of other mountainous parts of eastern America.

There is the legend of the tenant farmer who was a wizard and owned a magic book that was something like the Black Book already described. No other member of the family dared look into this wizard's book, and he himself could not read it until two of its pages had been glued together with blood. And once, while it was lying open on a table, it flew shut with a bang when no one was near enough to reach it.

Again the story of the husband and wife, one of them un-aware that the other was a witch, appears in the West Vir-ginia folklore. A man there was trying to churn, but a great swarm of cats appeared and climbed all over him and the churn, and he was unable to catch or drive them off. Just then a passing stranger dropped in and offered to help. He drew a knife and slashed off the right forepaw of one of the cats, whereupon all of them vanished. The grateful farmer invited the stranger to dinner and went to get his wife to prepare the meal, but he found her in bed, saying she was ill and could not cook.

Perhaps by that time the awful suspicion flashed into the

farmer's mind. "Put out your right hand and shake hands with this good man who rid us of the witch's spell," he ordered. When the wife refused, the farmer tore off the bedclothes and found that her right hand had been cut off. So he strangled her as the guilty witch.

This is only one of such weird tales—some similar in certain respects to those told in other parts of the country—that were believed in Virginia then and may be believed now by anyone credulous enough to do so.

❖❖❖ 6

CUNJERING IN GEORGIA

Georgia was the last of the American colonies to be established, in 1733. The story has been widely circulated and accepted that it was first settled by convicts. They were not convicts in the true sense of the word, although many had been released from the infamous debtors' prisons of London and other English cities. All were poor people, however, but all had been investigated as to their character before James Oglethorpe, Georgia's founder, and his associates arranged for them to emigrate to America. Nevertheless, being poor and ignorant and superstitious, the settlers doubtless did bring their beliefs in witchcraft to Georgia, although little is known of it compared to that in New England, Pennsylvania and some of the other original American colonies.

But after 1749, the year slavery was first allowed in Georgia and the great flood of Black slaves imported and sold to plantation owners was under way, the Devil began to be very busy in the new colony. This Georgia form of witchcraft was not especially different from that brought to other American colonies by the slaves, but it had a different name. The word was actually conjuring, meaning sorcery, but the Black people, learning English without the help of teachers, made it "cunjering," and a cunjer was a spell or curse.

Like the Blacks in other American colonies, and later in Louisiana, the cunjerers used charms, potions and incantations. In Georgia too, such ingredients as graveyard dirt, human hair and other rubbish believed to have supernatural powers were used.

The Black people had a deadly fear of cunjering. If one of them believed himself bewitched by it and could not rid himself of the spell, he would seek out a cunjer doctor—sometimes called a root doctor—to have it lifted. One Black man told as late as 1898 of how he was cunjered and what he did about it.

In May of that year, he said, while he was hoeing in the fields, pain struck him in both feet, especially the right one, and then spread over his whole body, finally reaching his head. He knew then that he was cunjered and went home to search for the cause of it. Under his front doorstep he found a little bag containing graveyard dirt, some nightshade roots and some "devil's snuff."

Nightshade is a vine which was brought to America from Europe and is common in many parts of the United States today. It has little purple flowers and bright red berries a little larger than currants. From it comes atropine, used in medicine, though nightshade berries are considered highly poisonous. Devil's snuff is a slate-colored powder found inside a large species of mushroom; its description sounds a good deal like common puffballs, most of which are nonpoisonous mushrooms.

The cunjered man lost no time in getting rid of the cunjer bag. He buried it in the middle of a well-traveled public road. Roads, especially crossroads, have much significance in witchcraft, particularly in African voodoo. The man then went home and sprinkled red pepper and sulphur throughout his house, both considered protection against cunjering. He added that with the coming of the next new moon he would get fresh roots of pokeberry, an herb which was also considered a protection against cunjer, make a tea of it and rub it on himself. Moreover, since his feet felt hot and he believed the cunjer had put a fire in them, he was going to see a root doctor to find out who had put the curse on him and to have the spell transferred to this cunjer enemy.

Cunjer bags like the one this man found were the most frequently used means of putting a spell on someone. Graveyard dirt was the commonest of the several ingredients a cunjer bag might contain. In order to be effective, graveyard dirt must be taken from the top of a dead person's coffin at midnight during the waning of the moon, after it is full. Black people in general avoided cemeteries at all times, especially at night, but it appears that the cunjer doctors had no such fear or that they hired someone brave enough to go there at the proper time to obtain the prized graveyard dirt.

Other ingredients in a cunjer bag included devil's snuff, a certain kind of worm, pieces of snakeskin, leaves or sticks tied with horsehair, a feather from a black owl, a bat's wing or a mole. The bag might simply be tossed on a victim's doorstep, hidden under it or buried somewhere near the house of the person to be bewitched.

One variety of cunjer bag which was not supposed to cause the cunjered person to die, but only to suffer great pain, contained snakeroot, an herb the Indians considered a remedy for snakebite, and needles and pins tied together with strands of hair obtained from the head of the person to be cunjered.

Of course the Black people sought protection from the dreaded cunjer. Red pepper and sulphur have been mentioned; also, if a person dared go by himself to a graveyard at night and got a bone from a dead person's skeleton, he was safe from cunjer if he carried it with him at all times. In addition to the pokeweed already described, rubbing the body with a potion made from the roots of an herb called pecune was also considered helpful.

Like the silver bullets sometimes used against witches in other parts of the country, the Georgia Blacks also had faith in silver as a protection against cunjer. Always having a piece of silver money in one shoe or the other, or in both, was supposed to ward off cunjer. Or, if a person was eating near someone suspected of being a cunjer doctor, he could ward off trouble by keeping a piece of silver money in his mouth while he ate or drank. Avoiding swallowing the coin at such times must have been a problem.

One smart Black man successfully tried an ingenious scheme to make money by pretending to be a cunjer doctor. A widowed Black woman who lived near Georgetown in southeastern Georgia had managed to save enough money to give her a reputation for being rich among the poverty-stricken people of that region. However, she held onto the money with a tight grip and refused all who pleaded for a gift or loan of cash. But when the cunning man heard that the widow was sick, he decided he could separate her from some of the money.

He made a cunjer of a small bottle into which he put graveyard dirt, some human hair and two small sticks, all

81

symbols of cunjer in Georgia. He buried the bottle near a path leading to the spring the widow and her family used, filled up and smoothed over the hole carefully and covered it with leaves. Then he went to see the widow.

He found her quite sick, with her anxious son and daughter at her bedside, all of which fitted in well with his plans. Pretending that he was a cunjer doctor who had heard of her trouble, he questioned the woman at great length about the symptoms of her illness, and what sort of pain she suffered, and then told her she had been cunjered.

This revelation made her feel worse than ever, but he told her the cunjer was somewhere nearby; if it could be found and destroyed, she would recover. For ten dollars, he said, he would find the cunjer, destroy it and break the spell and she would get well. If he did not find it, she would owe him nothing.

Ten dollars would buy far more than it does today, and in that poor area it was no small sum of money. But the scamp had made the widow feel desperate and she agreed to the proposal. To make her feel even more confident in his ability, he suggested that her son and daughter go along while he searched for the cunjer. As they set out, the false cunjer doctor carried an iron rod about a foot long, holding one end in each of his hands. If they approached the place where the cunjer was hidden, the rod would turn in his hand, he said.

He was too shrewd to go straight to the hiding place. First he walked around the yard in the opposite direction and nothing happened; the rod remained motionless. After a thorough search of the yard he went to the lot where the mules on the farm were kept, still with no result. Finally the swindler turned toward the path to the spring. As he approached the spot where he had buried the bottle, the rod in his hands began to turn. When they came closer, the rod seemed to become greatly agitated. The false cunjerer told the widow's son to go back and get a hoe and shovels. With these implements they dug until the buried bottle was discovered.

They took it back to the widow. Relieved of her fear and anxiety, she began to feel better almost at once and paid the deceiver his ten dollars. He gave her some roots to chew on that he said would restore her health completely, broke the bottle and buried it in the middle of a public road.

The widow did recover, and her faith in the false cunjer doctor was unshaken even when, in some way or other which the account does not reveal, his trickery was exposed. The incident adds further evidence that witchcraft often succeeds through psychology. And who knows but that an unscrupulous real cunjer doctor might have used the same method?

Whether or not the cunjer did really work, there were enough stories about its effectiveness to frighten the Georgia Black people into using every possible means to keep themselves free of its spells. And some of the occurrences had such serious results that it does not seem strange that these superstitious ones believed in cunjer and dreaded it.

One of the incidents concerned a Black man who was probably not a cunjer doctor at all, but consequently forced to become one. Bill Marshall lived in Georgetown, Georgia, a little west of the city of Augusta. One day while he was riding with another man in a wagon, his companion's hat blew off. Bill picked it up and handed it to the other man, who was taken ill a few days later and died.

Next, Marshall was drinking out of a well bucket; after his thirst was satisfied a Black woman drank out of the same bucket, and afterward she, too, died.

By that time the people of the village were sure Bill Marshall was a cunjer doctor. They were so terrified that they kept out of his way and had nothing to do with him. The owner of the plantation where he worked, in order to ease the fears of his other employees, discharged him. Marshall could find no work, so he went to live in a remote place and took up the cunjer doctor's profession.

Another serious cunjer incident took place on a plantation near Waynesboro, south of Augusta. An old Black man and his wife and son applied for work and were hired. The man and his wife insisted that they be given quarters as far away from the other plantation workers as possible.

This alone was enough to excite suspicion among the other Black plantation workers. Rumors began to circulate that the old woman, Hattie McGahee, was a cunjer doctor. It was said she could cure illness, relieve pain, foretell the future and cast spells that would either cause a man and his wife to separate or do the reverse and bring about a reconciliation between a separated couple. People also reported that Hattie McGahee used well-known symbols of witchcraft—familiars in the shapes of a dog and a cat, both jet black.

A young man working on the plantation, Henry Jackson, was in love with Laura Jones, but he had a rival, Joe Coleman. Jackson, having heard of Hattie McGahee's powers to bring about romance, arranged for her help in winning Laura Jones' affections.

Hattie McGahee went to work on Henry Jackson's behalf. She took some hair from one of her supposed familiars, burned it with sticks of sassafras and in some way administered the powdery ashes to Laura Jones, probably by sneaking them into her food.

On the same plantation lived Hosey Lightfoot, who also had a reputation as a root doctor who could arrange love affairs by cunjer. Joe Coleman, the rival for Laura, went to Hosey Lightfoot and enlisted his help. The battle between him and Hattie McGahee was on; cunjer bags containing graveyard dirt and bundles of small sticks were found on the paths leading to the houses of both rivals.

Other plantation hands became so alarmed that they refused to work in the same field with Hattie and her husband. One day the plantation owner found a large pile of cotton left in the cotton field. When he ordered the workers to remove it, they refused, saying that Hattie had put a spell on it. They even avoided walking on the same path that Hattie used.

Matters reached a climax when Hattie's black dog was mysteriously killed. Henry Jackson and some of his friends blamed Joe Coleman and his friends for it. The two groups met to settle the dispute and a bloody fight took place. One of the contestants, wielding an ax, mutilated Henry Jackson terribly, and Joe Coleman was badly beaten with sticks. Joe was not put completely out of action, and the authorities sent him to the prison chain gang for six months.

However, in spite of his serious injuries, Henry Jackson recovered, and while Joe Coleman was on the chain gang, working on the county roads under the supervision of brutal overseers, Henry married Laura Jones. But it appears that Hattie McGahee was not finished with her witchcraft. Joe Coleman's father was kicked by a mule soon afterward and died. The plantation workers saw it as cunjer by Hattie.

By that time the plantation owner had had his fill of the

trouble that the old woman seemed to have caused. He fired the McGahee family and that was the end of Hattie's cunjering, if that is what it was, on his property.

On the same plantation in 1896, cunjering caused serious trouble in which the owner himself and his brother were involved. A quarrel arose between Anna Bonney, a Black woman who milked the cows, and the plantation owner's Black cook, Jane Jackson. The two white men were having breakfast one morning when both became violently ill after drinking a little coffee. Since the plantation owner knew of no reason why any of his other Black employes should have a grudge against him, he questioned the cook, Jane Jackson, as to what might have gotten into the coffee. Jane said it must be the milk and that Anna Bonney had put a spell on it. The owner then questioned Anna, who claimed it was Jane who had put something in the milk so that Anna, her enemy, being the milk woman, would be fired.

The owner learned that pecune root, a powerful emetic that would cause violent stomach upsets, had somehow gotten into the coffee. But probably because the guilty person, in all likelihood one or the other of the two women who had quarreled, was frightened, nothing of the kind happened again and the owner did no more about it. However, trouble of another sort soon erupted. Chickens in the poultry yard began to die. Small bundles of sticks were found in the kitchen, and graveyard dirt was discovered strewn about in various places—both, as has been described, powerful cunjers in the eyes of the Black people. Then the water from the plantation well took on a peculiar taste. It was well known that a well could be cunjered by throwing graveyard dirt and devil's snuff into it.

The plantation owner may not have believed that a spell

could be put on the water in this way, but he did order that all water used for drinking and cooking be brought from a spring near the house. The unknown cunjerer retaliated by strewing bundles of sticks, graveyard dirt and devil's snuff along the path to the spring. Although the spring water was not affected, when a cow had a premature calf that died, the Black people laid it to cunjer.

As he had done in the case of the McGahees, the owner discharged both Anna Bonney and Jane Jackson. His own troubles then ended, but Anna Bonney appears to have paid with her life for her quarrel with Jane Jackson. Shortly afterward, Jane's husband, Joe, was seen making strange motions three times toward Anna Bonney's house. Anna, who was in the yard, fell to the ground in convulsions and died a few weeks later.

The foregoing two stories were written by the plantation owner. There are many other cunjer tales, but the facts in these two seem credible enough. The effects of some of the African forms of witchcraft, of which cunjer in Georgia was one, are extremely difficult to explain.

❈ ❈ ❈ 7
SATAN'S MISCHIEF
IN OTHER COLONIES

The archives of New Jersey, Delaware and North and South Carolina contain no records of witchcraft trials or witch hunts of any consequence. For the two original New Jerseys, East and West, and Delaware, the chief reason probably lies in the type of people who lived there.

Except for some in East or northern New Jersey, there were few Puritans in these colonies, and since they were in a minority they had little chance to stir up witch hunts. The people of New Jersey and Delaware were chiefly farmers, simple, good people who had no interest in persecuting suspected witches in court.

Most did believe in witches and wizards, however. Old women who were scolds, peculiar in their ways, thin with angular features and large noses, who did much spinning for no apparent reason, smoked black pipes and kept black cats, were always suspected. Many people believed they could avoid trouble by giving witchlike people food and shelter when it was asked for.

One case, however, in which generosity to a suspected witch seemed to be of benefit concerned a child sick and near death. The family invited a supposed witch of the neighborhood in for a cup of tea. The old woman undressed the child and blew in its face, and it recovered.

On the other hand, some believed that giving anything to a suspected witch was dangerous. A cow belonging to a New Jersey settler became ill of a mysterious malady. The farmer used the remedy already mentioned as a cure in other colonies for livestock thought to be bewitched. He snipped off a piece of the cow's ear. But before he went into the barn to perform the operation, he warned his wife to give nothing to anyone. While he was in the barn, two strange women knocked at the farmhouse door asking for food. They were so innocent looking that the wife gave them something to eat. That night the cow died.

New Jersey settlers, like those of many other colonies, believed witches harmed livestock by shooting bullets of hair into them. They also employed the widely used method of making cream turn to butter in a churn that seemed bewitched—putting a hot horseshoe into it. One unique substitute for this remedy was to burn the likeness of a horseshoe into the bottom of the churn. One New Jersey witchcraft legend tells of a suspected male witch who bore the scar of a horseshoe forever on his face when a hot one was dropped into a churn.

Some New Jersey colonists believed they could punish a suspected witch by getting some piece of cloth belonging to her and burning it. The witch would then also suffer burns; there are tales of how some were badly burned in this way.

North Carolina developed slowly, and once it did expand, its planters and farmers were too busy battling a series of tyrannical English royal governors to try suspected witches for their lives. In South Carolina it was much the same, except that the difficulty for its early settlers, mostly in the tidewater country near the seacoast, lay in cultivating the marshy, malaria-ridden land in order to stay alive; in fact, for some time England had to send ships loaded with food for the colonists of South Carolina. Thus in this colony too, fighting the Devil by searching out and trying his earthly representatives, the witches, did not attract the attention of the settlers.

The question of whether New York ever had a witchcraft case is one which may be answered either yes or no. The colony and later the state of New York have always been noted for their freedom and liberality toward their inhabitants. No law against witchcraft has been found on their statute books. And during the Salem witchcraft delusion, New York offered a refuge to a number of suspected or accused Massachusetts Bay witches who were able to escape. The best known of them were a wealthy Salem merchant-shipowner, Philip English, and his wife. They were accused and held in Boston Prison for trial. Friends in the city staged a daring rescue of the Englishes and had horses waiting on which the two rode for their lives to a warm welcome and safety in New York City until the delusion ended.

Three witchcraft cases did appear on Long Island, however, but this is a question as to whether, until 1664, the island was actually a part of Dutch New Amsterdam or of Connecticut. Early settlers migrated there from Connecticut; they were largely Puritans and thus witch hunters. On that basis, although there were Dutch Long Island settlers too, Connecticut considered it a part of that colony. But no doubt Peter Stuyvesant had other ideas about its ownership.

Yet when Elizabeth Garlick of East Hampton was brought before the magistrates of that village under suspicion of witchcraft in 1657, she was sent to Hartford, Connecticut, where Governor Winthrop presided over her trial. The evidence against her was so flimsy that the jury acquitted her. However, Goody Garlick was extremely unpopular in East Hampton because she was a gossip with a sharp tongue. Returning there was the last thing she and her husband wanted. Lion Gardiner, founder of Saybrook, Connecticut, came to the Garlicks' aid. He had bought an island—today Gardiner's Island, still owned entirely by one of his descendants—off the eastern tip of Long Island. Goody Garlick had worked there as a house servant before her marriage. Lion Gardiner offered the Garlicks refuge on his island. They accepted and lived there the rest of their lives.

A second Long Island witchcraft case took place in Oyster Bay in 1660. Mary Wright, old, poor, ignorant and apparently friendless, was accused of being a witch. The Oyster Bay magistrates were puzzled; a witchcraft trial was something they knew nothing about. So they sent her, not to Connecticut, but to Massachusetts Bay. Their decision seems queer, since Massachusetts had no claim to Long Island, but their reasoning appears to have been that the Puritans there were the foremost experts in detecting witches.

Old and helpless as she was, Mary Wright turned on the General Court in Boston which tried her and fought her judges with the fury of a battle-scarred alley cat. She charged the court with thirsting for blood and advised the members to repent of their evil ways. She seems to have succeeded in intimidating them at least into acquitting her of witchcraft, though they did banish her as a Quaker.

The last known case of Long Island witchcraft took place

in 1665, the year after the English conquered New Amsterdam. The new English colony of New York asserted its authority over Long Island, and when Ralph Hall and his wife of Brookhaven were accused, they were taken to New York City. Even though there appears to have been no New York law against witchcraft, witchcraft they were tried for before a jury of six Long Islanders and six New Yorkers. Perhaps for that very reason, the Halls were acquitted.

However, although the four colonies first discussed had no witchcraft trials and New York, even if Long Island is considered part of it, had none of great consequence, it should not be thought for a moment that witchcraft beliefs did not flourish in all of them. Their people, like those of the other eight colonies, had their superstitions, their witchcraft legends and, particularly in the South, suspected witches and wizards, with their supposed powers of curing illness or putting evil spells on people and livestock.

Here again, many similarities to witchcraft beliefs in other colonies are found. Some vary slightly, but are basically the same. There is little published witchcraft lore in New York, New Jersey and Delaware, but the Carolinas, particularly North Carolina, abound in it.

For example, here are some of the North Carolina beliefs that resemble those of other colonies:

—Rubbing oneself with a grease distilled from corpses to become a witch, change into the form of an animal or be able to fly

—The evil associated with black cats, owls, toads and other creatures

—Belief in witch marks and that one must sell his soul to the Devil to become a witch

—The white witch, using her powers for good, and the black witch, doing evil

—The use of salt to keep witches away from a house; also, nailing a horseshoe over a door or putting a broom across a door

—The use of images with pins stuck in them to put spells on people; in North Carolina images of dough were used in addition to rag dolls and waxen or wooden images, and the dough was then roasted or buried or had pins stuck into it

—Putting a horseshoe into a churn

—Use of silver bullets fired at a witch's image to break her spell or kill her

—Different from Pennsylvania hex marks, yet for the same purpose—painting a barn red to keep witches out

—The ways of outwitting witches that many people use today to ward off bad luck or bring fortune—throwing a pinch of salt over the shoulder or carrying a rabbit's foot

—Belief that witches ride horses at night (the familiar tangled mane in the morning as proof that the witch used it as a stirrup to mount)

These are only a few of the superstitions and ways of protection against witches that were common in one way or another, not only in the Carolinas but in other American colonies.

In North Carolina an old man protected himself against witches' spells for forty years by keeping a silver dollar in his mouth night and day. Once the figures on the coin wore off he replaced it with a new one. A most inconvenient method and dangerous at night, but the man believed it worked.

The belief that witches milked cows was widespread in

colonial America. The North Carolinians had a bizarre belief in how it was done. The witch did not have to enter the barn; she put a new pin in a towel for each cow she wanted to milk and hung it over her own door. Muttering incantations, she would seize the towel by the lower fringe and make the motions of milking, and lo! out would squirt the milk.

A witchcraft story from the North Carolina mountains tells how a witch forced a man to atone for a crime. The man, whose name was Johnson, went to a notorious witch to be cured of kidney stones. She told him that she knew he had cheated a cattle buyer of several hundred dollars and he must return the money before she could help him. The guilty man did so, but whether the supposed witch cured him is not known, for the story somehow got out and Johnson's reputation in the community became so bad that he had to move elsewhere.

In the Carolinas, as in Georgia, "conjure" ("cunjer") doctors were known; one near the village of Clayton, North Carolina, was supposed to have cured a Black man's swollen feet by drawing live frogs from them. Graveyard dust was a favorite ingredient for charms and other witchcraft practices all over the South; in the Carolinas it was called "goofer dust." And as in other colonies, Carolinians believed witches fired bullets of hair into animals to bewitch them.

In central North Carolina, according to well-substantiated facts, in a grove about ten miles from Silver City is a completely bare path in the shape of a perfect circle, forty feet in diameter and about a foot wide. Those who believe in the supernatural claim that the Devil comes there at night, pacing around the circle as he devises new ways to do evil in the world. Residents of the region say the path has been there as long as anybody can remember. Inside the circle a variety of wiry-stemmed plant called wiregrass grows. Outside it are other grasses and moss. But nothing, so the story goes, will grow in the path. It is said that people have put sticks and stones secured by anchored strings across the path, but by the next day they are always gone.

Adding to the supernatural nature of the Devil's Tramping Ground, as it is called, is a local belief that no birds will nest near it and that wild game shuns the vicinity. Once, it is told, when a hunting party came toward the path, their dogs would no longer continue the trail they were following and slunk behind their masters as if seeking protection.

Several explanations for the existence of the Devil's Tramping Ground have been offered. One is that the grove was once used by the Croatan Indian tribe for their war dances and that as the warriors circled, their feet wore the bare, circular path. Why, then, after all these years, has the trodden path remained bare, while inside it and out vegetation grows? This has been explained by a legend that a great Croatan chieftain, killed in battle, was buried inside the circle and that the Great Spirit kept the path around the grave bare. Some scientists who did research on the subject said that the earth in the path is heavily impregnated with salt and therefore nothing will grow there. It is difficult to believe that a perfect circle of salty earth could exist, when inside and outside it the earth is fertile.

Perhaps the most logical explanation, though still not a good one, is that an old-fashioned molasses mill once stood in the center of the circle. Many mills of this type were operated by horses or mules plodding in a circle around them and attached to them by long poles that turned the mill wheels. But since the mill, if there was one, is long gone, why did the earth remain bare?

The Devil's Tramping Ground was a great attraction for visitors in bygone years, but more recently its fame seems to have waned. However, in 1967 a group of Explorer Scouts in Garner, North Carolina, decided on a daring expedition to challenge the sinister reputation of the place. They not only planned to go there in the dead of winter and spend the night, something that according to legend no one had ever done and survived, but they chose the time of the full moon, when ghosts, witches and Satan himself are supposed to be most active.

The date was set for Saturday, February 25. As it approached, a few timid ones in the group dropped out, but of its thirteen members, nine showed up, actually eager to find out what Satan might have in store for them at the Devil's Tramping Ground.

The day was bitter, with the thermometer thirteen degrees above zero. The nine brave ones, with their adult leader, drove the short distance to Silver City and got directions nearby to their objective.

It stood about fifty yards from the highway in a wooded area. They found the circle practically as the legend described it—bare except for a few small patches of an unusual type of grass, though pretty well covered with dead leaves, which they scraped aside.

They made camp inside the circle and dined on stew made over a roaring fire. The full moon rose, it became even colder and the wind howled, but in spite of the eeriness the campers —perhaps to show each other they were not frightened—told witch legends around the fire.

By eleven o'clock all were in their tents, some already asleep, when suddenly they were disturbed by several loud explosions. These did not frighten them, however, since they recognized the noise as firecrackers and moments later heard the roar and squealing tires of a hastily departing car. Some jokers in the vicinity had decided to give the boys a good scare. The rest of the night, with a record low temperature for that region, passed uneventfully. If, during the small hours, Satan too defied the intense cold to take a few turns around the circle, plotting evil deeds, none of the adventurous party heard or saw him.

One eerie North Carolina mountain legend concerns 2,600-foot Brown Mountain. For over a century mysterious lights have been seen hovering over it at night. They rise over the mountain, disappear and then appear again. The story reminds one of the many UFOs—Unidentified Flying Objects—reported in recent years from many parts of the United States and thought by some to be coming from some inhabited place in outer space.

John Foster West, in his book *You Take the Highroad: Along the Blue Ridge Parkway*, tells of the lights and of attempts to explain the mystery. He says, "In 1913, D. B. Starett of the U. S. Geological Survey visited Brown Mountain seeking the source of the lights. His theory, ultimately, was that they were caused by the headlights of locomotives—but they continued to appear after the railroad was washed away by a flood. In 1922, George N. Mansfield, also from the U. S. Geological Survey, concluded that the air in the Catawba Valley refracted lights as a liquid does and that 47 per cent of the lights were from automobile lights; 33 per cent from locomotive headlights; 10 per cent caused by brush fires, and 10 per cent were stationary lights.

"But the mountain dwellers scoffed at this explanation also. Other theories are that the lights are will-o'-the-wisps (marsh gas), phosphors [substances that give off light when subjected to radiation], phosphorescence (fox fire), other chemical reactions, steam from moonshine stills, and Andes lights (electrical discharges).

"Of course there are other explanations some natives accept readily. There is the one about Posy Slewfoot, the mythical moonshiner who brews incandescent moonshine. Or better yet, the eerie lights are caused by the lantern of a ghostly slave who forever searches for his master, lost somewhere in the mountains."

The lights are still often seen, and on the Blue Ridge Parkway amidst the towering peaks of the Great Smoky Mountains, there is an exhibit about the Brown Mountain lights. But no one has ever found an explanation for them to satisfy everybody.

THE BELL WITCH OF TENNESSEE AND MISSISSIPPI

As settlement of the American colonies pushed westward after the last of the colonial wars ended in 1763, Englishmen, Scotch-Irishmen and some Germans were the chief migrants into the Appalachian Mountain country. They brought with them witchcraft beliefs and superstitions, many of which still prevail among the mountaineers in that high, rocky country, split by narrow valleys, that takes in the western part of the Carolinas, Virginia and Maryland, much of West Virginia and the easternmost parts of Kentucky and Tennessee.

In the latter part of the eighteenth century, settlers in large numbers moved even farther west, and it was in the rolling country west of the mountains in northern Tennessee, not more than thirty or forty miles north of today's city of Nashville, that the most amazing Tennessee witch story had its origin.

In the early part of the nineteenth century, John Bell and his family lived there, in a large and substantial log cabin in Robertson County. Since this family had suffered the mysterious persecutions of an evil spirit for a number of years, the apparition became known as the Bell witch.

The story is a long one and contains so many unbelievable events that it might be dismissed as pure legend if it were not supported by so much evidence in the way of dates and the names of witnesses concerned in it. The tale is especially fantastic because of the many kinds of evil the supposed witch worked.

The story, spreading over a number of years, was not published until 1894, some seventy-five years after the strange events began. William Bell, one of the family who lived through the persecutions of the apparition, kept a diary in which he recorded what happened. From the entries in this diary he wrote an account of it in 1846. Upon his death the manuscript came into the hands of his eldest son, Allen Bell.

The author of the published account became intimately acquainted with Allen Bell and his brother Joel. Hearing about the manuscript, he was intensely interested and asked permission to write it up for publication. Joel was willing, but Allen refused. However, after the death of the last member of the family who had been alive while the Bell witch was active, Allen granted the permission and the story was printed.

The Bell witch first made its presence known in 1817. John Bell was walking through his cornfield when an animal appeared that looked like nothing he had ever seen before. He shot at it, but missed, and the creature escaped. A few days later another member of the family, Drew Bell, saw what looked like a very large wild turkey. He crept up to get within shooting range, but the bird took alarm and flew away. As it rose into the air, Drew Bell saw that it was far larger than any turkey he had ever seen.

Next, one of the daughters, Betsy Bell, was walking outside early one evening with one of the family's grandchildren. They came upon a little girl dressed all in green, swinging from the limb of a great oak tree. Betsy knew all the neighboring children but did not recognize the little girl as any of them and, afraid there was something queer about it, went back home without investigating further.

The Bells had a Black slave named Dean, who was married to a slave who belonged to another family in the settlement. Dean was in the habit of going to visit his wife each evening, and finally he reported to the Bells that night after night he had seen a large black dog trotting ahead of him in the road. The dog always went up to the door of the cabin where Dean's wife lived and then vanished.

All these were queer happenings, but they troubled no one until one night when the Bell family heard loud knocking on the door and walls of their house. They investigated and found nothing. Later that night, however, the family was awakened by a variety of sounds like dogs fighting, chains being dragged over a floor and rats gnawing at woodwork. The noises seemed to come from the room where the younger boys slept. John Bell got up, lit a candle and went into the room, but nothing was there and the noises had stopped. Just then, however, he heard his daughter Betsy scream from her room: "Something is after me!"

The next day John Bell suffered one of the ailments typical in witchcraft lore when a spell has been put upon someone. His tongue became stiff, and it was as though there was a stick of wood crosswise in his mouth. He pushed the food out of his mouth when he tried to eat.

Tennessee was God-fearing country and the great tide of religious revival that took place early in the nineteenth century had spread to that region. The revival period was marked with the establishment by traveling revivalist ministers of camp meeting grounds where devotional services were held with sermons and hymn singing. Two of these revivalists, James and William Johnson, had founded Johnson's Camp Ground near the village. John Bell decided the best thing to do was to seek religious advice, and he told James Johnson all that had happened.

Mr. Johnson prayed to the Lord to end the Bells' troubles. This seems to have enraged the evil spirit, for as soon as the Johnsons were in bed that night there was a frightful racket somewhere around their house.

A little before the Bells' troubles began they had taken a woman lodger from North Carolina, where the Bell family had lived before coming to Tennessee. From the story it appears that the Bells were not particularly anxious to have the woman there, but she had been so insistent that they took her in. She called herself simply Kate.

It seems possible that Kate was the witch who caused the troubles, and later on some people suspected her, though at first no one did, including the Bell family. Kate professed herself to be a Christian and a devout Methodist.

The witch's next move was to go after Betsy, the youngest of the Bell family's daughters. She and a young man of the village, Joshua Gardner, had fallen in love, but no sooner was their engagement announced than Betsy heard a soft, melancholy voice from some invisible source warning her not to marry Joshua. Betsy then began to have attacks of hysteria that hampered her breathing so that she would nearly suffocate. At the same time, she complained that something was sticking pins into her.

By that time the Bells and their neighbors were convinced

that a witch was at work. Thereupon, some people declared it must be the Bells' mysterious lodger, Kate. Then something happened that made them wonder if they were mistaken.

Another Kate, Mrs. Kate Batts, who was very fat, had some queer ways. During a revival meeting at the camp ground, Mrs. Batts suddenly sailed in and planted all of her two hundred pounds on top of a man attending the meeting.

"Let him up!" someone shouted as the poor victim struggled to free himself. "Don't you see he's suffocating?"

"Yes, blessed Jesus," Mrs. Batts replied, "let him suffocate! He's coming closer to the Lord."

The victim was released before he met the Lord, but the incident caused many people to believe that Mrs. Batts was the witch working her evil in the village, though there was no definite evidence against her.

James Johnson's attempt to gain the Lord's help in the problem not only caused him trouble, but it failed to stop the Bells' afflictions. The witch kept on tormenting Betsy. The girl often received a hard blow on her cheek or had her hair pulled until she screamed, although she saw no one near her.

The apparition did not confine its attentions to the Bell family. A number of people held conversations with it, though it was always invisible. At first the voice was only whistling sounds, but soon those who tried to communicate with it began to make out distinct words, though they were uttered in a low whisper. Through these conversations the witch's mischievous sense of humor was revealed, and the Bell family was always the target of its cruel jokes.

John Bell himself was finally able to establish communication with the mysterious apparition. He asked, "Who are you?"

"I am a spirit," came the reply. "I was once very happy, but have been disturbed."

"Why are you disturbed?"

"I am the spirit of a person who was buried in the woods nearby, and the grave has been disturbed, my bones disinterred and scattered and one of my teeth was lost inside this house [the Bells' house], and I am looking for that tooth."

One of the Bell sons then recalled how, several years before, he and some others had been roving the woods when they came upon a grave which had been opened, and where bones had been strewn about. They assumed the place was one of the Indian burial mounds of the region.

One of the boys had picked up the jawbone of the disinterred skeleton and brought it back to the Bell house. For no good reason he had thrown it against the wall and knocked out a loose tooth in the jaw. It fell through a crack in the floor and disappeared.

John Bell decided the missing tooth must be found, since that was what was troubling the witch. If it were restored, the apparition would surely go away and let the family alone. He and his sons tore up the floor and searched diligently, but no tooth was found. The witch then gave a laugh and said the story was all a joke.

The apparition had not finished plaguing the Bells. A little later it said, "I am the spirit of an early immigrant who brought a large sum of money with him and buried it. I died without revealing the secret, and I have returned for the purpose of making known the hiding place. I want Betsy to have the money."

Probably the Bells thought the witch had repented of torturing Betsy and wanted to atone for it by giving her the money. Yet when they asked where the treasure was hidden, the witch teased them by refusing to tell where it was. Finally, however, the apparition said it was under a large flat rock at the mouth of a spring in the northwest corner of the farm. Armed with shovels and crowbars, the male members of the Bell family rushed to the spot, pried away the stone and dug a deep hole, but found no treasure. That night the invisible spirit came to the house, laughing at how it had deceived them. Presumably the Bells did not share its glee over the mischievous hoax.

The witch did tell one tale that came true. When John Bell planned to make a journey back to his old home in North Carolina, he heard the witch's whisper: "Do not go to North Carolina. A young lady from Virginia who is rich and elegant is coming here. If you stay home you can win her."

Since John Bell's wife is not mentioned in the story, he appears to have been a widower, and the witch's prediction might have dissuaded him from making the journey, but by that time he believed in nothing the witch said. He laughed at her and went to North Carolina. While he was away a beautiful and wealthy young lady from Virginia did come to the village, but she went home before John Bell returned.

Now the witch inflicted more torments upon Betsy Bell than at any time before. The young girl began to go into trances in which she appeared to be lifeless. The witch seemed bent on forcing Betsy not to marry Joshua Gardner.

The grudge against John Bell was revived also. The trouble with his mouth reappeared; but the apparition then denied that it was tormenting him. It said Kate Batts was responsible, and some people felt more certain than ever that the fat woman was the real witch.

There are many other tales about the activities of the Bell witch: how it assumed four different identities, not shapes, since it was never visible except possibly in the guise of the strange animal John Bell had seen before the trouble began, as the huge turkey, as the mysterious little girl in green or as the dog that the slave Dean had seen; how the apparition beat within an inch of his life a detective who had come, probably from the city of Nashville, boasting how he would solve the mystery; and other fantastic doings. Finally, the apparition does seem to have appeared again to Dean, since it had made it known that it hated him, claiming he smelled bad. Dean saw the thing several times after that in the guise of a black dog, but sometimes the animal had two heads. Dean took to carrying an ax and a charm called a witch's ball wherever he went.

John Bell was so distressed over all the family's ills that he thought of moving away. Meanwhile, his condition became worse. The doctor gave him some medicine, but the witch appears to have replaced it with a potion of its own. When Mr. Bell came to take the medicine, it had given way to a smoky-looking vial, half full of a dark liquid. One of the family dipped a straw in the vial and wiped it on a cat's tongue. Instantly the animal leaped into the air, whirled around and fell dead. The family threw the vial into the fire and it disappeared in a flash of blue fire.

Soon afterward poor John Bell died. The witch then announced that it was leaving, but would return in seven years. It appeared at first to have kept its promise to go, for Betsy

Bell's health returned, but then she heard the witch's voice again warning her not to marry Joshua Gardner. Betsy was so terrified that she broke off the engagement.

Another version of the story, less well authenticated, and carrying it on from Tennessee to Mississippi, deserves a brief description. According to this legend, after the Bell witch ceased its persecutions in Tennessee, members of the family remained in the house there for several years, but finally moved to Mississippi, settling near Batesville in Panola County on the road to Oxford.

These members of the Bell family were comfortably located in a two-story, double log cabin, but to their dismay the Bell witch was already there when they arrived. Though no one had seen the mysterious apparition in Tennessee, it had been generally assumed that the witch was a woman. In Mississippi, however, it soon became plain that it was a man.

The head of the family was John Bell, a son of the older John Bell who had died in Tennessee. Among his children was a pretty young girl, Mary. One day the spirit appeared to Mr. and Mrs. John Bell, and announced in a man's voice that he was in love with Mary and wanted to marry her. The Bells were horrified and Mr. Bell told the apparition that under no circumstances would he allow the marriage with Mary to take place.

Apparently the witch then appeared, still invisible, to Mary and tried to persuade her, though nothing is known of what was said. But after that Mary became depressed and assumed an almost trancelike state. She would wander about inside and outside the house like a sleepwalker. She became deathly pale and had a faraway look in her dark eyes. She went earlier to bed each night, and rose later in the morning.

A day came when Mary did not get up at all. That night the eerie wail of a screech owl was heard from the cedar trees just outside the house. By that time Mary had a high fever and by midnight was in a raving delirium.

Panola County, with its rolling countryside, is still today one of the less thickly populated parts of Mississippi; then it was wilderness. Mr. Bell announced he would go for a doctor, though the nearest one was an hour's ride away. The witch's voice said it could get a doctor much more quickly than Mr. Bell.

The Bells decided to take the witch's advice. Within an hour the doctor arrived. He said he had been summoned by someone shouting outside his window. He shook his head after he had examined Mary, and said that medicine could not cure her, since the illness was caused by the state of her mind and nerves. However, he added, she was young and strong and ought to recover if the Bells were patient and did nothing to upset her. Before he left, he gave them something that could be used to put her to sleep if she began raving again.

Mary lay in bed for a month, her eyes straining into the distance as if she were trying to see something. The Bells kept the affair secret and told the neighbors nothing.

One night when Mrs. Bell, sitting by the bed, was leaning tenderly over her daughter, Mary pushed her away and sat up. "Mama," she whispered, "I see him . . . at last . . . and I think I'm going to love him."

Then Mary Bell died.

There were no undertakers or hearses nearby. The Bells

made a coffin for Mary and put it on a wagon. As the vehicle rumbled over the rough dirt road toward the cemetery, a great black bird appeared, hovering over it, with a bell around its neck that tolled mournfully. The bird remained there until the coffin was lowered into the grave and covered up. Then it soared high into the sky and disappeared; and the witch never annoyed the family afterward.

So goes the legend of the Bell witch in Mississippi.

❀ ❀ ❀ 9
VOODOO IN NEW ORLEANS

New Orleans in the nineteenth century was fertile soil for workers of magic. The city was a mixture of races and nationalities. Until Americans flocked in after the Louisiana Purchase in 1803, the French predominated among the white people. They founded the city in 1718 and held it until 1763, when France ceded it to Spain. Spanish settlers came, but New Orleans' character remained French, and in 1783 France regained it. The citizens who were of pure French or Spanish blood were called Creoles. They were aristocratic, mostly wealthy, with fine houses, carriages, stables and Black servants.

Blacks formed more than half of New Orleans' population in the early years of the nineteenth century. They were a mixed lot. In color they ranged from pure black to yellowish or tawny color, down to those who were so nearly white that indeed many did pass for white people. The Blacks included those of pure African blood; mulattoes, one of whose parents was black, the other white; quadroons, who had only one-quarter black blood, and octoroons, only one-eighth black.

Some of the Blacks were slaves and some were free. The latter or their ancestors either had been freed by their white masters or had managed to escape from the plantations where they worked as slaves. A good many of these free Blacks were well-to-do, even rich. They lived in fine houses and, although they did not mix socially with the whites except on certain occasions, they had their own elegant society. Some owned slaves themselves.

Among the other nationalities were a good many Germans, some other Europeans and a few Americans, mostly traders or adventurers. There were also a good many Indians, chiefly Choctaws and Chickasaws. Most of this hodge-podge of people lived in what was then the center of the city, the *Vieux Carré* or French Quarter. It nestled within the great bend of the Mississippi River which gives New Orleans its name of the Crescent City.

The French Quarter was a crowded rabbit warren of structures, large and small. Many of the buildings lining the narrow streets of the French Quarter were beautiful. Their upper stories had open balconies ornamented by railings of delicate, lacelike, exquisitely wrought metal which overhung the *banquettes,* as the sidewalks were called.

There were also a number of Catholic churches in the French Quarter. They represented a strange inconsistency in the life of the Quarter. The people of the section were largely Black or partly Black. Practically all of them attended mass regularly in one of these churches; yet at the same time, most of them practiced voodoo.

Voodoo originated in Africa and was brought to the New World by slaves. It came into New Orleans from the island of Hispaniola, which today includes Haiti, long a stronghold of voodooism. The Spaniards who controlled the island

111

brought in many slaves from there while they occupied New Orleans.

The Spaniards had converted their slaves in the West Indies to Catholicism. The Blacks attended mass and observed the Catholic religion, but at the same time they not only clung to their own religion, voodooism, but borrowed many of the Catholic rites and incorporated them into their voodoo ceremonies. The Catholic Church was outraged, of course, since voodoo was considered a religion of the Devil himself. Yet priests and other Catholic clergy, unable to stop the introduction of Catholic practices into voodooism, preferred to keep the Blacks as Catholics, hoping to get them to shun voodooism.

Voodooism attempted to work both good and evil. Witch doctors, the succession of powerful voodoo queens in New Orleans and female witch doctors known as voodooiennes were used by the ignorant and superstitious, as well as by the intelligent people of both races, to cure all sorts of ailments and diseases. The voodooists, men and women, had a wide knowledge of herbs, simples, roots and plants which they used in potions to cure the sick. They were so expert at this that a great many residents of New Orleans depended upon their skill.

Some of the voodooists used their supposedly magic powers only for good; others used them for both good and evil. A voodoo doctor, queen or voodooienne might claim to be able to put curses on people and also to lift curses from those who believed they had been bewitched. The curse might be used only to cause some person's enemy to have bad luck or to suffer pain or it could, usually in return for a large sum of money, even kill. Those who had a fatal curse put on them often did die.

The heart of voodoo practices was the *gris-gris*, a French word meaning a charm or amulet. There were scores of different *gris-gris*, each designed for a certain purpose—to bring success in love, to cure ailments, to put a curse of one kind or another on a person, to bring luck and to "unwitch" those who believed they had been bewitched and had had a curse laid on them.

There were so many kinds of *gris-gris* that it would be impossible to name them all, and they were made of the strangest ingredients imaginable. Just to name a few that were used, there were dried or powdered frogs, toads, lizards, snails, earthworms and snakes, broken bottles, eggshells, grease, sugar, dried herbs, red pepper, coffee grounds, nails, the feathers, legs and claws of roosters and hens, beef tongues, snake fangs and alligator teeth. As was the case with black witchcraft in other regions, one of the most prized ingredients was "grave dirt." Many little shops in the French Quarter sold materials for making *gris-gris*.

Gris-gris that were signs of a curse were tiny coffins, crosses of death and strange powders, usually left on the stoop of the accursed man or woman. Other *gris-gris* might be carried with a person, especially those designed to bring good fortune. Sometimes they would be hidden in some nook or cranny as near as possible to the altar of a Catholic church, or placed before the image of a particular saint in the church or a saint's picture in a house. Another favorite place for them was in front of or behind a tomb in a cemetery.

There were counter–*gris-gris* intended to keep a person from harm by witchcraft. If an evil *gris-gris* were left on someone's doorstep, a remedy was scrubbing the stoop with brick dust. To keep out evil spirits, a ring of salt might be sprinkled around the whole house, or horseshoes nailed over the door or Catholic holy pictures put up inside.

Voodoo ceremonies in New Orleans were secret, but there are many descriptions of them. The biggest and most important of them all was held on St. John's Eve, June 23, the night before Midsummer Day and the saint's birthday. This, too, was a ceremony borrowed from the Catholic Church, though it is doubtfult if the good saint would have approved of what went on each St. John's Eve in a secret grove on the shore of Bayou St. John, just north of New Orleans.

A huge crowd always attended. Before the ceremony began, they gorged themselves on chicken and cake and drank too much rum and anisette. By the time the reigning voodoo queen appeared, most were very drunk and in a state of wild excitement.

The queen wore nothing but a few handkerchiefs and a blue cord around her waist. She went into a weird, trance-like dance and then placed a picture of St. John on the ground. The half-crazed crowd knelt and knocked three times on the ground for Faith, Hope and Charity.

Next the queen made a signal and the spectators stripped off their clothes and ran into the bayou. The water was no more than five feet deep, but some would be so drunk they would fall down, be made to rise and drown.

Indoor ceremonies were even more secret, but a fifteen-year-old boy attended the initiation of four candidates into the cult and described it. It was held during the reign of a New Orleans voodoo queen named Dédé.

A crowd of members was on hand. They all had white handkerchiefs tied around their foreheads, though the women also had the headdresses all Black women wore—a bright-colored handkerchief of cotton or silk Madras called a *tignon,* fashioned so that it had seven points, all sticking straight upright to bring luck.

At each end of an oblong table stood a cat, one black, one white, which looked alive, but were stuffed. On a keg in the middle of the table stood a cypress sapling about four feet high. Behind and above it was a black doll, its dress decorated with mystic symbols, wearing a necklace of snakes' fangs from which dangled an alligator's tooth encased in silver.

An old Black man was beating a wooden drum with a sheepskin head, while a Black woman belabored the drum's sides with a turkey or buzzard's leg, and nearby a young man shook a gourd filled with pebbles.

The candidates came forward as Dédé appeared, and she sprinkled them with a liquid from a calabash. As she made a signal to the old man beating the drum, he darted to a sort of casket and drew from it a huge live snake.

In most forms of voodooism the snake is considered the supreme spirit—the Vodu—and is sometimes believed to be the Devil himself in the form of a reptile. Snakes, caught in the nearby swamps, were almost always used at voodoo ceremonies. If they were deadly moccasins or rattlesnakes, the fangs and the sac containing the poison could be removed.

The man with the snake brandished it overhead, talking and whispering to it. The four candidates crossed their arms and formed a circle around him. He made the snake raise its head upright about ten inches and passed it over the candidates' heads and around their necks, repeating the name of the African sect they were joining: "Voodoo Magnan."

Thus the candidates became voodooists and, as usual at all

voodoo ceremonies, there followed an orgy at which all danced crazily and went into trances.

In addition to its rites and ceremonies, voodooism was supposed to work magic. One of the best-known voodoo queens, Lala, used special methods for accomplishing different things. If a woman came to her in fear that her husband was going to leave her, Lala would tell her to light three candles and put them on a table, stick her husband with a pin until blood flowed, mix some of the blood with black ink and write the man's name on a sheet of paper nine times. Then the woman was to make a promise to a powerful voodoo spirit named Ozoncaire to pay him for keeping her husband with her.

She would pay the debt by pouring a bottle of whiskey into the mouth of a sheep's head and taking it out on a country road at midnight wearing only a red nightgown and a red cap. The sheep's head was to be placed under an oak tree, with the words: "Ozoncaire, that's for you." The woman was then to walk home backward in the middle of the street, being careful not to step on a *banquette*.

The candle lighted at the start of the affair was one of many used in all kinds of voodoo ceremonies and casting of spells. White, green, blue, red and black ones were all used, each for a different purpose. Black candles, symbolic of death, were used when someone was to be killed by voodoo magic, and for other evil purposes.

Lala's recipe for making someone go away included a black candle. It was melted and the wax kneaded like dough. Then it was rolled into a ball. The hated person's name was written on a piece of paper, four times forward and four times backward, and placed in the middle of the ball. Next, some pins were stuck into the ball and it was thrown overboard from a ferry in the middle of the Mississippi River. The person anxious to be rid of another was then to snap his or her fingers and say, "Saint Expédire, make him go away quick!" When the victim left, a pound cake was to be laid in front of the saint's statue in Our Lady of Guadelupe Church.

It is most doubtful that there ever was a saint named Expédire (a French word meaning to speed things up), but the voodooists may have given the name to some saint's statue in the church to suit their purposes.

Lala claimed she could drive a person insane. This spell was expensive, costing five hundred dollars, but she did put in a great deal of work to accomplish the evil deed. She would write the victim's name nine times on a guinea hen's egg and put it in a hole in a tree. Then she would pray to the tree once a week for five months. When the victim went crazy, she had to pay a voodoo saint for it. He had the improbable name of Tit Albert and an equally improbable fondness for soup plates. Lala would compensate Tit Albert by burying a soup plate under the tree.

Here again the suggestion crops up that Lala's victim was made to know the curse had been placed on him and that it was fear that drove him out of his mind.

She also claimed she could restore an insane person to his right mind. This difficult feat also cost five hundred dollars. Lala would sit the insane person in a chair, split a white dove in half and put the two halves on top of his head, letting all the blood run down over his face. She then washed the patient's face in a white bowl, put three nickels in the bowl and threw it in the river. This was supposed to cure the insane person.

Lala also had methods enabling a person to win a court

117

case, to bring a runaway girl back home and to keep people from being fired by their bosses. She had a *gris-gris* that would bring a victim quickly to his ruin, and she could also show people how to sell themselves to the Devil.

A voodooienne, Julia Jackson, who practiced her art in the twentieth century, had several ways of killing people. She used her power so profitably for over thirty years that she became rich, bought a great deal of property and had an automobile in which she went into the country districts outside the city, where business was especially good. There was a story, believed by many people in the French Quarter, that she had once killed a man by making two strokes on his forehead with a red pencil.

Another of her methods was to catch a rattlesnake, kill it and hang it in the sun to dry. Then she would write the doomed person's name on a piece of paper and put it in the snake's mouth. Once the snake had dried up completely and decomposed, the victim too would dry up and die.

A third way was to kill a rooster, chop off its claws and head and take them to a cemetery; put a black candle on the beak, lay it in front of a tomb and bury the feet in back of the tomb; light the black candle and pray for an hour that bad luck would come to the victim; and, finally, dig up the rooster's feet and bury them and the beak in his yard. Julia Jackson claimed the bewitched person would die within a week. This is another of the roles that cemeteries, tombs and graves played in voodoo.

Often, when a witch doctor or voodooienne was summoned to treat a sick person, the doctor would say the person had been bewitched by putting snails and frogs inside him. One voodoo legend concerns a mulatto woman who was trying to steal another woman's husband.

The man was faithful to his wife and told the mulatto to go away. The mulatto was evidently a voodooienne. That night when the man got home, he was feeling ill. When his wife put him to bed, she noticed that his face was flushed and that there were little yellow spots behind his ears. She called in a witch doctor, who said the man was bewitched and had snails inside him. He told the wife that if she could get her husband to spit them up he might recover. The husband, after several attempts, threw up three big snails and a little green frog, which all instantly disappeared when they struck the floor. The terrified wife ran screaming out of the house. When she got up the courage to go back, she found her husband gasping for breath, with blood running from his nose, and very soon he died.

Some of the stories have it that bewitched people would go into fits, small snakes would come out of their mouths and they would die. Others told of spiders coming out of bewitched people's ears before they died. A girl, walking down the street, had some dust thrown in her eyes. She was blinded, and the explanation was that the evil *gris-gris* was from the completely decomposed body of a snake dried in the sun.

All these things sound like sheer nonsense, and they may have been. Yet voodooism could never have flourished as it did in Africa, in the West Indies, especially Haiti, and in New Orleans for so many years and, at least to some extent, today, unless a great many people were convinced that voodoo did work. One example of the power some witch doctors had over the people is that of the famous Dr. John in New Orleans.

One who had never seen Dr. John and passed him on one of the little narrow streets of the French Quarter during the nineteenth century would have been forced to stop and gape at him, even though there were many other queer-looking characters in the Quarter at that period.

Dr. John was an old man, just how old no one knows, but before he died he claimed to be over a hundred. Yet he did not look old. He was a gigantic Black man and his appearance was so repulsive that, gazing at him, no one could doubt that he was capable of every evil. His face was disfigured by colored scars in the shape of snakes that seemed to writhe down from his temples to the corners of his mouth.

The scars were tattoos. Dr. John claimed he was a prince of Senegal, on the West African coast along the Gulf of Guinea. His father, king of his tribe, had his son's face marked in that way according to royal tradition. So said Dr. John and he may have spoken the truth.

His costume was equally bizarre. It added to his mystic appearance by being entirely black except for a white shirt front with frills on it. And he wore a beard that further enhanced his professional appearance—that of a voodoo witch doctor.

Dr. John said he had been taken from Africa to Cuba by a white man, whether as a slave is not clear, although in New Orleans he was a free man. If he was a slave in Cuba he must have escaped, for he told of working in sailing vessels and then coming ashore in New Orleans to work on the wharves along the Mississippi.

It was at that time, he said, that he discovered he had magical powers. Since African voodoo was brought to New Orleans by slaves owned by Frenchmen or Spaniards who came to start cotton or sugar cane plantations outside the city, Dr. John, as a professed African prince, was thoroughly familiar with the cult's mystic practices. When he found that he could use his powers and get money for doing so, he became a witch doctor and took the name of Dr. John.

Dr. John's new business paid well. Not only the ignorant, poor people of the French Quarter were glad to part with money for his good and evil *gris-gris* and the telling of fortunes, but also many of the elegant wives of wealthy Creoles, part-Blacks and the Americans who were settling the area north of the French Quarter. These clients, most of them women who came discreetly veiled to Dr. John's house, were eager to pay large sums of money for his services.

He soon grew rich, bought property, lived in a fine house and owned slaves, all of them women. Some of these slaves he married, performing the ceremony himself in a mystic voodoo rite. He boasted that he had fifteen wives and over fifty children.

If one wanted good luck, Dr. John had a charm that would bring it. If a person wanted harm to come to an enemy, Dr. John would, for a large fee, put a curse on the enemy that would take care of him. The old witch doctor knew how to lift a curse placed on a person by some other witch doctor or voodooienne, "unwitching" the bewitched one. Aging ladies came to him to have their youth restored. Those who were ill could be made well again. A young man in love or an old one with young ideas could make sure a hoped-for romance would succeed by going to Dr. John, paying the large sum of money the doctor demanded and receiving a love charm that could not fail. The *gris-gris* prepared for success in love was a human skull wrapped in human hair and placed in a bag of talcum powder.

One strange story, in view of the actions of the stone-throwing demon, Lithobolia, in far-off New Hampshire, was

121

that many people were struck by showers of stones near Dr. John's house. Several times he was arrested and charged with throwing the stones, but he was always discharged for lack of evidence.

How did Dr. John get away with what seems to be such foolishness? For one thing, he used astrology in his work. For centuries, people have used and believed in astrology. The most famous of all astrologers, Nostradamus, made a number of predictions for the future that came true with startling accuracy. Even today astrology flourishes and many thousands of people have complete faith in it.

Like Nostradamus, Dr. John also used divination or second sight. It is fairly well proved that some persons have this gift to a greater or lesser extent. ESP (extra-sensory perception) has been scientifically tested and found to work for some people. Thus Dr. John, especially in his fortune telling, relied partly on astrology and second sight.

Of much greater importance to him, however, was his vast store of knowledge about his clients, particularly the wealthy people who came to obtain his aid. These rich men and women all had Black servants, and Dr. John employed scores of them to eavesdrop, watch all that went on in the big houses and report everything to him. Thus when some wealthy lady called on him, he would amaze her by telling her secrets about her life that she thought were unknown. Once Dr. John had such visitors convinced that through magic no secret was safe from him, they had full faith in his powers.

Faith can do great things. Accomplishment of difficult objectives is far easier for a person who has faith in being able to succeed in them. Such people would be quick to believe in Dr. John's *gris-gris,* spells and other witchcraft. They

122

seemed to bring fortune to many who, bolstered by faith, had actually gained it themselves. The lover armed with one of the witch doctor's charms would be confident and bold.

As for the curses Dr. John put upon enemies of his clients, it has been quite well established that in one way or another the victim was made to know the spell was on him. Thus an accursed person would fall prey to his own mind; he became crazed with fear, and his mind did the rest. No doubt Dr. John always found a way to let a superstitious victim know there was a fatal curse on him. This would also explain the voodooienne Julia Jackson's deadly magic. And just in case the curse failed to work, it could be explained that the victim had managed to find someone with a *gris-gris* powerful enough to lift the curse.

How did Dr. John bring youth back to aging ladies? Sometimes, no doubt, by making them *feel* younger. But voodooists always had a wide acquaintance with herbs, simples, other plants and roots. Today ladies spend billions of dollars annually on cosmetics to improve their skin and complexion, to iron out wrinkles and make gray hair vanish, as well as paying large sums for "face lifts." Who knows but that Dr. John had his own stock of cosmetic ointments, oils and potions to do the same thing?

This explanation also applied to those who were ill and came to Dr. John for aid. As a master herbalist he must have had a medicine cabinet filled with remedies he concocted himself. After all, many of our modern remedies came, originally at least, from herbs, roots, plants and trees —such as digitalis, the powerful drug used in cases of heart disease; quinine, the best known means of controlling malaria; and many others. The practice of medicine in the nineteenth century cannot measure up to the wonders of

modern medical science, but who knows whether some of
Dr. John's mystic remedies were not just as good as, or better
than, many used today?

Of course, like all voodooists, Dr. John relied upon a good
deal of mumbo-jumbo—the strange rubbish used in many
gris-gris, incantations, mystic symbols, colored candles and
the like. Those who visited his house were awed at the sight
there of snakes, lizards, scorpions that looked alive but were
dead and the skulls of animals and human beings. Where
he got the human skulls no one knew, but grave robbing
doubtless flourished in the New Orleans of that day.

Dr. John had his rivals, but none as successful as he.
One competitor was a Dr. Yak-Yak, who told fortunes and
offered to heal ill people. He was well acquainted with poi-
sons as well as healing potions. Someone persuaded him to
put a death curse on an Italian fruit dealer who was coming
to him to be treated for rheumatism. Dr. Yak-Yak gave him
a potion to drink, but the fruit dealer became suspicious. He
had it analyzed by a chemist, who found it was a deadly
poison. Dr. Yak-Yak was arrested, but at his trial he was let
off with a fine, perhaps because he had influential clients
who were ready to get him out of his trouble.

The story of another witch doctor seems unbelievable, but
it is on the records. Dr. Jack, another of Dr. John's rivals,
had had great success with the love charms he manufactured.
His *gris-gris* for successful romance was a beef heart which
was perfumed and ornamented with toads' feet, claws of
fighting cocks with spurs attached and ribbons of colored
satin. It was very expensive.

Dr. Jack seems to have had faith in the charm for his
own purposes, for he always slept with one hanging over
his bed. One night the charm fell from its cord and landed

on Dr. Jack's face. He woke with a start and, so the story goes, was so terrified that he lost his senses and died within three days. He is supposed to be the only voodoo doctor who literally frightened himself to death.

One other strange character among the New Orleans witch doctors came after Dr. John's time and practiced into the early years of the twentieth century. He was a great fraud, but this did not prevent him from making so much money that he had his wife's teeth set with diamonds.

This man who claimed to practice voodoo was really a dentist by the name of Joseph M. McKay, but in New Orleans he called himself Dr. Cat. He did not confine his practice to the city, but set up a mail order business there, selling "magic" candles, *gris-gris* and advice on all kinds of problems throughout the United States. Post Office inspectors went after him for using the mails to defraud, but he got out of New Orleans just ahead of them. They finally caught up with him in Birmingham, Alabama, in 1914. At his trial he said he was 127 years old, though he looked like a man in his twenties. Dr. Cat was convicted, served two years in a Federal prison and then disappeared.

The witch doctors had followings who considered their magic to be wonderful indeed, but to most people of the French Quarter and to many who lived outside it, their powers were as nothing compared to those of the voodoo queens. They reigned in succession in New Orleans and their story is an interesting one, especially that of the most famous of them all—Marie Laveau.

❁ ❁ ❁ 10

MARIE LAVEAU, THE GREATEST VOODOO QUEEN

There were many voodoo queens in New Orleans, but none so great and powerful as Marie Laveau. She not only obtained almost absolute power over most of the city's Black people, but also had a tremendous influence with wealthy Creoles and other whites, including ladies of the highest social standing, prominent businessmen, politicians and city officials.

Marie Laveau was a mixture of white, Black and Indian, a tall, distinguished-looking woman, beautiful, with black, curling hair, dark skin with a reddish tinge and black eyes that could gleam with animal-like ferocity. She was a free woman.

Marie was born, probably in the very last years of the eighteenth century or the first ones of the nineteenth, in humble circumstances, became a devoted Catholic and for a long time had no connection with voodoo. In 1819 she was married to Jacques Paris, also poor and a carpenter. The marriage lasted only a short time before Jacques Paris vanished and was never heard of again.

Marie followed the usual custom of a woman whose husband had died, calling herself "the Widow Paris." Since she had a talent for hairdressing, she began to go into the houses of wealthy Creoles and other whites to do the ladies' coiffures when they were preparing for some important social event.

Just as today, hairdressing salons were hotbeds of gossip, and Marie Laveau heard things one would never have thought these rich ladies would ever breathe a word about. Marie had a way with her that invited confession, and indeed many of these women yearned to ease their minds by telling their troubles to someone. In Marie, they had selected a confidante who was shrewd and intelligent and had smart business sense, and who stored the secrets away in her mind, not to be forgotten.

It might be a supposedly white woman in whose family there was a strain of Black blood and who lived in dread that it might be discovered and ruin her social career. There were families in New Orleans in which an insane member was kept locked away from the outside world—and who knew when and where madness might crop out again in another of the family? Also, a great many of these ladies knew their husbands had married them only for business reasons and took their pleasure with beautiful quadroons who lived in ease in little cottages in the French Quarter. A wife who knows her husband is unfaithful needs someone in whom to confide her heartache. And Marie also came to know which public officials were stealing money paid in taxes by the citizens of New Orleans. All these things and others were soon to be of inestimable value to her.

She took another husband, though there was no official marriage ceremony. He was Louis Glapion, a quadroon

127

who came from Santo Domingo. During the years before Glapion died they had fifteen children.

Hairdressing paid well, but Marie began to realize that she could use her intelligence and the secrets she knew to make much more money. She took up voodoo.

There were a number of voodoo queens and witch doctors already in New Orleans, the most powerful one then being the elderly Sanité Dédé.

By 1830 Marie Laveau was a voodooienne, one of the minor voodoo queens. In her cult she made a sweeping change in the way voodooism was practiced. Already, voodoo was using some Catholic rites; nevertheless, it was a religion by itself, and its god was not the God of Christianity and Judaism, since voodooists believed the snake, the Vodu, was the instrument through which the Devil worked magic arts. But Marie brought in other rites of the Catholic Church— statues of Catholic saints, prayers and incense. In her voodoo cult the Devil was no longer worshipped and she called her people Christians.

In spite of Catholic disapproval of voodooism, Marie remained a Catholic as well as a voodooienne, and often went with the beloved priest Père Antoine of the Cathedral of St. Louis to visit the sick, especially during the terrible epidemics, usually of yellow fever, that swept New Orleans from time to time. She seemed to have no fear of contracting the dread disease.

Nevertheless, Marie Laveau did not give up the equipment used in voodoo. It was highly valuable to her in impressing those who came to her for aid in their problems. She used the snake and the black cat of voodoo ceremonies. At the secret meetings of her cult there were candles, drinking of freshly killed fowls' blood, dancing of African origin, drinking and orgies. The making of *gris-gris* and potions, fortune telling and the placing of spells were the most profitable part of Marie's new trade.

Women whose hair she dressed now came to her for *gris-gris* to bring fortune, to have those fortunes told and to have spells placed on enemies. As Marie's reputation grew, others came—men and women, young and old. Wealthy men could pay large sums of money for her services, but she did not refuse help to the poor. They paid what they could or, better still, became part of her corps of spies, for many worked in the big houses as servants for both Creoles and white Americans.

When Marie Saloppé, then the reigning voodoo queen, died, Marie Laveau was determined to succeed her. It is said that she brought Marie Saloppé to ruin before her death by putting evil spells on her. Marie Laveau was ruthless in the way she went after the throne of principal voodoo queen. She got rid of some of her rivals simply by threatening them, for she could be a menacing figure. When she met the defiant rival on the street, Marie would beat her unmercifully until the rival voodooienne either promised to give up the rule of her own cult or to serve under Marie as a sort of sub-queen.

If these means failed, there were always the *gris-gris*. Marie had built up such a reputation for success with them that many of her rivals were frightened lest they be overcome by a spell so powerful that they could not make it harmless by one of their own. Some left the city and some died—by Marie's bewitchment, it was believed in New Orleans. And at last no one disputed Marie Laveau's position

129

as the reigning voodoo queen of the city. Voodoo, which until then had been disorganized, was now unified under her rule.

Marie had many enemies, of course. Charges were often made against her for her witchcraft practices, but these cases seldom reached the courts, and if they did they were dismissed for one reason or another. Her power over officials was so great that she never feared imprisonment.

Marie also used her power to get others out of trouble with the law. One day a wealthy man of a prominent family came to see her. His son had been arrested for a serious crime and the evidence against him was so strong that it seemed the young man must go to prison. Somehow, said his father, Marie must get his son freed. She promised she would try.

The day of the trial was set. At dawn that morning, Marie entered the Cathedral of St. Louis, knelt at the altar and prayed for several hours. Under her tongue she had three Guinea pepper beans, the variety from which the hot red pepper we use today is obtained.

Next door to the Cathedral was the Cabildo, or city hall, where the trial was to be held. When Marie left the church, she crept into the trial chamber and put the three pepper beans under the judge's chair. That day the judge dismissed the charge against the young man.

How was it done? Had Marie's prayers to the Christian God she worshipped so faithfully been answered? Had the *gris-gris* of the peppers under the judge's chair caused him to find the young man innocent? Or, perhaps more likely, was it Marie's strong influence with the politicians of New Orleans?

This feat of Marie Laveau's made her reputation even

greater. The young man's father gave her a cottage in the French Quarter. It was better than the lodgings she and Louis Glapion occupied; best of all it had a large yard, which she had surrounded with a high board fence so no one could see what was going on inside. There Marie held secret meetings of her cult. Glapion died in the cottage in 1835 at the age of 66, and Marie remained there, never remarrying.

She was not above using tricks when there was something she needed. If some Black woman was a servant in a house where Marie did not have a spy, she would steal out late at night and leave one of the dreaded death-curse *gris-gris*—a doll stuck with pins or a ball of wax covered with feathers—on the woman's front stoop. Inevitably, the woman would come knocking at Marie's door the next morning, almost paralyzed with fright and begging the voodoo queen to remove the curse some unknown enemy had placed upon her. Marie would oblige and in return had one more spy to add to her long list.

Marie's cottage was a busy place. Ladies of high degree, rich businessmen, politicians and officials, as well as the Blacks of her voodoo cult, swarmed there to ask advice, buy her *gris-gris* that would bring them luck or have their fortunes told. Marie Laveau, through her spy system, knew so much about people in New Orleans that everyone was awed at her mind-reading skill. In addition, she had her keen intelligence and perhaps a gift of what appears to have been a certain amount of second sight. Marie grew rich.

She did not forget the secret cult meetings which enabled her to keep her power over the superstitious members of her voodoo cult. A witness who was said to have discovered a way to peer into the cottage yard described one of these night meetings.

On the ground was spread a white sheet with lighted candles around its edges. In the middle of the sheet were five empty bottles. The members of the cult, all stark naked and holding bottles of rum or whiskey, would dance around the sheet, sprinkling it and each other with the liquor. Then they would begin a dance, singing songs in the strange Creole language, which was based on French, but contained so much queer dialect that a Frenchman would have had difficulty in understanding more than a few of the words.

Marie Laveau, the only one who was dressed, presided over the ceremonies, standing in the middle of the sheet. She was queenly in a long blue dress with a full skirt and a beautiful *tignon* with seven upstanding points, and wore bracelets and hoop earrings of gold.

Marie directed the dancers' movements. Her snake—a very large one—would be brought in and she would make it crawl over the dancers' legs. By that time they were wildly excited and their movements grotesque. As the drums' beat grew more rapid, the people would take mouthfuls of liquor and blow them at each other, bob up and down and spin around so fast that some collapsed from dizziness and had to be revived with whiskey.

Then Marie would pick up the snake, wrap it around her shoulders and begin a writhing, snakelike dance of her own, twisting and shaking, but never moving her feet.

Another even more carefully concealed meeting place for the most secret gatherings of Marie's cult was a house on a lake outside the city. Here the members were allowed to give full sway to Hispaniola voodoo—the killing of fowls and animals and the drinking of their warm blood, and a bizarre dance in which they carried torches and imitated the movements of snakes and alligators, hissing and crawling on the ground, hopping and croaking like frogs and screeching like owls. All night long, bonfires blazed around the house and along the lake shore.

Thus did Marie keep her cult faithful to voodooism and maintain her position as the reigning queen of voodoo in New Orleans.

Prisoners in jail held a strange fascination for her, especially those condemned to be executed. She could walk unchallenged into any jail and talk with the inmates. She was given credit for one hideous incident in which she was believed to have tried to save two condemned men from death. Both were to be executed at the same time. They mounted the twin gallows, the nooses were placed around their necks and the traps were sprung, but as they plunged toward eternity both ropes broke. The men fell to the ground, bruised and injured, but alive. However, if Marie did try some spell to save them and it worked, her efforts were in vain, for the two men were brought up to the gallows again, new ropes were fitted and they were hanged once more, this time permanently. But in the French Quarter people believed Marie's magic had saved them the first time.

She did prevent one hanging, though not by magic, and it merely saved the condemned prisoner the ordeal of death on the gallows. A man from a distinguished Creole family, apparently so drunk that he scarcely knew what he was doing, killed a harmless old man one night. After a long trial, in which the best lawyers fought to save his life, he was finally sentenced to hang.

While he was awaiting execution, Marie Laveau often visited him. On the day before he was to be hanged, she asked if there was some favorite food she might bring him for his last meal. He spoke of gumbo, the thick soup of meat, okra and other vegetables, all highly seasoned, that is so popular in New Orleans.

"I will make you a gumbo such as you have never eaten before in your whole life," Marie promised him.

She certainly did. At dawn, when the guards came for the condemned man, they found him on the floor of his cell. He expired before they could get him to the gallows. Marie Laveau had for once cheated the hangman, though not with *gris-gris*. The man had eaten the gumbo she brought him.

Whether Marie actually did cheat the gallows on one other occasion is a question, but she got the credit for it. Joseph Bazar's wife was unfaithful to him, and when he caught her with her lover he killed the man. At his trial he was convicted of murder and sentenced to hang.

As usual, Marie Laveau was a constant visitor to his cell before the time set for his execution. What they talked about or what she may have promised to do to aid him is unknown, but the day of his execution dawned, the guards came and took him to the gallows in the prison yard and the noose was put around his neck. All that remained was for the prison warden to give the signal. . . .

At that moment a horseman galloped madly into the prison yard with a shout that caused the springing of the trap to be halted. He bore a commutation of the death sentence, signed by Governor Henry Clay Warmoth. Had Marie Laveau had a hand in that last-second saving of Joseph Bazar's life? The people of the French Quarter believed she had.

The story of Marie Laveau's last public appearance at a voodoo rite was described in the *New Orleans Times* for March 21, 1869. A human corpse was displayed at one end of the room. Marie, dressed in red and yellow, with a *tignon* on her head, stood on a dais and set the dancers moving in a circle by singing a wild Creole song, echoed by the participants, who also beat time with their hands and feet. In the center of the circle was a basket filled with half a dozen snakes, all hissing and lifting their heads above the top of the container.

Marie was now over seventy years old and the cult had decided she should retire. However, for a number of years afterwards, people still came to her house, seeking the aid of her magic arts.

Then came a change. Marie Laveau renounced all connection with voodoo and became devoted solely to the Catholic Church. Thus, on June 16, 1881, when she died peacefully in her sleep at the age of about eighty-five, she was buried in the consecrated ground of the St. Louis Cemetery.

Many weird legends sprang up about the manner of her death. There were even reports that she was not dead at all, and these persisted into the first two decades of the twentieth century. The reason is that at least one and perhaps two Queen Marie Laveaus reigned after her death.

The first was one of her daughters, Marie Glapion, who took the name of Marie Laveau. Less is known of her reign than of her mother's, but it was far less distinguished and she indulged in some practices her mother never would have stood for.

As for the third Marie Laveau, her real name was Malvina Latour and there is no proof that she was the daughter of the second Marie Laveau. Even less is known of her than of her predecessor.

The first Marie Laveau may have worked evil through some of her magic, but the good she did far outweighed it.

How much of her success was due to her witchcraft is doubtful except that through it she gave her clients confidence in themselves as well as in her that helped them to overcome illness and spells cast upon them by other witches and witch doctors.

One may believe what one likes about Marie Laveau's magical powers, but no one can deny that she was the greatest of all the New Orleans voodoo queens.

THE WEIRD WITCHCRAFT
OF NEW MEXICO

The wife of a ranch owner in New Mexico decided she wanted to become a witch. In order to join the Devil's cult, she was told she must commit some evil upon the person she loved most. She loved her husband dearly, but she wanted so much to become a *bruja* (the Spanish word for witch, pronounced "brooha") that she bewitched him and he soon became ill of a liver ailment.

Like others who were not aware that their spouses were witches, the New Mexico lady did not know that her husband was already an *hechicero* (sorcerer or male witch, pronounced "etchisayro") and that he had found out that his wife had bewitched him. So he bewitched her.

One day the newly created witch had been out in the fields cutting wheat with a scythe. Just as she got back to the patio of the ranch she went into convulsions and slit her throat with the scythe. The blow was so powerful that she nearly cut her head off, and of course died.

She had suffered her punishment at the hands of her husband, but even in death she had her revenge. Within a month the husband also died of the liver disease her bewitchment is said to have brought upon him.

Belief in witchcraft spread much farther west than the Mississippi River during and after the eighteenth century. The story of the sorcerer–ranch owner and his witch-wife is only one of dozens from New Mexico, for example. Indeed it is fertile country for witchcraft beliefs. New Mexico, in former days, was almost all wild, with the deserts and mountain ranges that are still there. Most of the early settlements clung to the banks of the long Rio Grande or were near it. They were small and surrounded by lonely countryside where it was easy to believe that strange things might happen. The people were largely either of Spanish ancestry, Indians or mixtures of the white and red races, most of them ignorant, credulous and superstitious.

Separation of New Mexico from Spain came in 1821, although it did not officially become a territory of the United States until 1846. The Spaniards brought with them their own witchcraft traditions from Mexico. The Indians had theirs.

It was a different sort of witchcraft from that of America east of the Mississippi in many ways, yet there are similarities that help to prove how ancient witchcraft is. As in all forms of witchcraft, religion had its part in the West. In New Mexico the Catholic Spanish-Americans turned to their religion when they thought they were threatened by witchcraft. Beliefs in America of how witches appeared, disguised themselves and worked their magic vary considerably. Yet people everywhere believed in the ability of a witch or of Satan himself to appear in the forms of animals, birds or reptiles.

However, there were differences in New Mexico. Many people there were convinced that a witch could appear as a ball of fire leaping great distances from place to place. The idea that witches could ride broomsticks or animals or fly through the air seems to belong chiefly to the original American colonies.

In New Mexico people believed that a witch in the form of a ball of fire could be trapped. A person abroad at night who saw a leaping ball of fire had only to draw a circle in the road. The circle had the power to pull the witch into it, where she would be unable to leave. In the morning she would change back to her natural form, but would still be unable to leave unless someone pulled her out of the circle.

Chata was an old woman who lived in Tome, a town not far south of Albuquerque. Everyone in her neighborhood believed she was a witch; in fact, this region of Valencia County seems to have been a veritable nest of witches and sorcerers.

Tome was also the home of Juan Chávez, a very poor but well-liked man who was always willing to share what he had with other needy people. One day in 1897, one of his friends who lived some distance away sent word to Juan that if he would come there he could have a cow that the friend owned.

Juan set out and night fell before he reached his destination. In the darkness of the desolate region he saw a ball of fire down the road ahead of him. He leaped off his horse and drew a circle in the road. The ball of fire disappeared.

Juan reached his friend's house, stayed overnight and started back with the cow tethered behind his horse. When he reached the circle he had drawn, he recognized an old woman sitting there. It was Chata.

He greeted the supposed witch and asked what she was doing there. All she would say was, "Here I am."

"It is very hot," Juan said. "Let us go along to Tome."

"I can't go from here unless you will give me your hand," Chata replied.

Probably because he feared she would bewitch him if he refused, Juan Chávez did so. As has been said, he was a good-hearted man, and in any event he would not have to fear Chata's magic thereafter.

The magic circle was used not only to entrap a witch, but to kill her. This could be done only in a house where a boy named Juan lived. If a strange animal or bird entered such a house, the boy would take off all his clothes, turn them inside out and put them on that way. He would then draw a circle near the doorway of the house. With that, if the animal or bird was indeed a witch, it would disappear. The next morning the witch would be found in her house in her natural form, dead.

Another way of proving the guilt of a suspected witch was to entice her into a house where a cross of needles had been put over the doorway and a broom behind the door. If the woman were really a witch, she would be as helpless as the one within the magic circle in a road and could not leave the house until the charms against her power were removed.

Several methods were used as protection against bewitchment. The favorite one among these credulous people was the use of their own religion. A witch feared a cross, and even making the sign of the cross would repel one. Another protection when a witch threatened someone was to say, "Mother of God!" or "Blessed be the sweet names of Jesus, Mary and Joseph." Strong as these people's belief in witchcraft was, religion was stronger. The Bible teaches resistance against the wiles of the Evil One and witches' power was supposed to come directly from the Devil.

140

Nevertheless, there were charms used against witches in that region of New Mexico that had no connection with religion. There was nothing religious about the magic circle. And people carried charms that were not religious symbols. One was a piece of a certain wild gourd; another a piece of a burnt nut called the *gachana*.

Charms or no charms, witchcraft persisted in the region of New Mexico around the mountain town of Manzano, south of Albuquerque, and Bernalillo in the Rio Grande valley, north of Albuquerque. Perhaps the most revolting of the witch stories, however, comes from the mountains of the northern part of the state. Among the family of a young man who lived there were several uncles and aunts. On certain nights these relatives would drive out of town, using a horse and buggy. The young man's curiosity as to where they went and what they did became so overpowering that one night when he knew they were going out he tied himself under the body of the buggy.

The uncles and aunts got into the vehicle and drove off at a frightening speed. From his concealment their nephew could not tell just where they were heading, but at last they stopped at a house in a lonely region that stood in a draw, a kind of drainage basin whose walls concealed the place.

When his relatives entered the house, the young man untied himself and crept up under a window. Peering in, he saw a room filled with witches, including his uncles and aunts, all dancing and capering about. Suddenly a huge billy goat entered the room through a door. He walked in a circle around the witches, who all kissed his tail.

The goat then left and in slithered a big snake. As it crawled slowly around the circle, the witches stuck their tongues out to be kissed by the serpent's own forked tongue.

The snake then glided away and in came four men, all in black, carrying a large box. From it they drew a dead body. Like so many vultures, the witches swarmed in and began to eat the corpse. The terrified young man could watch no longer. He ran back to the buggy and fastened himself under it again. Shortly afterward, his relatives came out and drove home.

This unbelievable story illustrates the connection between witchcraft and the Devil, as well as a similarity to voodoo. Witchcraft credits the goat as one of Satan's favorite disguises when appearing on earth. The snake, or Vodu, is of course the ruling symbol of voodooism. The serpent who successfully tempted Eve to eat of the forbidden fruit in the Garden of Eden, according to the Old Testament's Book of Genesis, is not directly referred to as the Devil. But the meaning of the snake as Satan in disguise becomes plain, and in the Book of Revelations of the New Testament this reptile is identified as Satan.

As for the hideous flesh-eating orgy the young man is said to have seen, cannibalism has been connected with pagan religious ceremonies for centuries. Their particular occurrence, if it did happen, could have been brought to New Mexico from Mexico. There, in bygone years, human sacrifices were offered to the Mexican Indian god Huitzilopochtli. The victims, generally captured enemies or slaves, were put on an altar before the images of gods. A priest would cut the victim's breast open, tear out his heart and sprinkle those at the scene with blood, after which the rest of the body was eaten by all.

There is also a possible connection between the eating of human flesh in witchcraft orgies and the Devil. One of the most horrifying pictures ever done by a noted artist hangs in the famous Prado Museum in Madrid. It is by the great Spanish painter Goya, much of whose work is on religious subjects. The painting is called "Satan Eating His Son." One glance at it is enough to give one nightmares.

Was the corpse in the orgy that the young man witnessed killed by some witch's spell? There were several methods of doing so. One, greatly feared by the people in the region of New Mexico where witchcraft flourished so rampantly, is ancient and widespread—the evil eye. Gypsies are reputed to be expert at this practice, and since they are roving people, belief in the evil eye has followed them in their widespread wanderings. Fear of it is strongest on the Italian island of Sicily. There, today, people wear charms to guard themselves against the evil eye. Those who practice it fix their victims with a malignant, piercing gaze which is considered to be fatal.

The superstitious ones in New Mexico believed in the *mal ojo,* or evil eye. Among those thought to possess its death-dealing power were some of the Indians of the region. The story is told of two young boys who went to a fiesta held in honor of one of the Spanish Catholic saints. As usual at such celebrations, the people danced, ate and drank, and many stands were set up to sell food, drink and souvenirs. The two boys went up to a fruit stand operated by Indians. Some of the red men fixed the boys with the terrible gaze of the *mal ojo* and both fell sick and died.

Another New Mexico way of killing people or otherwise harming them is probably as old and common elsewhere as witchcraft itself—making dolls of rags or wax which are the images of the intended victims, and sticking pins in them.

143

In the town of Tajique lived an old woman whom many of the people believed to be a witch. She was said to use the image method of working evil.

A woman in the town fell ill of a strange malady which could not be cured. She was sure the supposed witch had put a curse on her and had the old woman arrested and brought to trial. Since the sick woman knew her insubstantial tale of having been bewitched would not be strong enough evidence to convict the accused witch, she brought a friend, who told the court a fantastic story.

The friend claimed that one day when the accused witch was not at home, she had gone there. In one corner of the room was a pile of rags. Underneath them, said the witness, was a cross lying on a heavy robe which she could not lift, but was able to push aside. Underneath it was a hole in which lay a mass of writhing snakes.

In case this testimony was not enough to prove witchcraft, the sick woman's friend had a second story. She said she had gone one day with the accused witch to a lake near town. There the witch, who was a fat woman with a hairy upper lip resembling a mustache, suddenly changed herself into a dog and ran away.

The justice of the peace presiding at the trial seems to have been a sensible man who put no trust in the witness' weird story. He found the accused witch not guilty.

A much more puzzling witch story concerns a poor sheepherder, Manuel Lujan, who lived on a ranch along the Rio Grande in southwestern New Mexico. One day the ranch owner sent Manuel with a companion to drive a flock of sheep north through the valley to Valencia County, over a hundred miles away and in the countryside around Manzano,

144

which seems to have been witch-infested. One night the two camped at the Valverde River crossing. They had just lain down to sleep when they saw a small animal creep up and begin eating a piece of their beef. Manuel's companion grabbed his gun and shot the creature, but he only wounded it and it ran off.

After breakfast the next morning, the two men struck the trail leading to their destination. They followed it for a few miles and then were surprised to notice footprints in the sand that looked like human ones, yet they were in the midst of arid desert, inhabited only by a few Navaho Indians who always rode horseback when they went anywhere. As they followed the footprints they came upon a pool of blood a short distance farther on.

Both of them were frightened, but they continued to trail the footprints until they reached a river crossing, toward which the footprints led. It was decided that Manuel should cross, while his companion went on with the sheep to Valencia County.

On the other side of the river, in a cottonwood grove, Manuel found an old woman bleeding badly from a shoulder wound.

"Was it Indians who shot you?" he asked.

The woman glared fiercely at him. "No! *You* shot me!"

Manuel was bewildered. "I shot no one," he said.

"Then it was your companion!" the old woman cried.

Manuel then knew she must be a witch who had raided the camp at Valverde in the shape of an animal. He feared she would bewitch him, and in the hope that she would not if he helped her he took her to Los Lunas in Valencia County and left her to have her wound dressed. Then, with all speed, he hurried on to join his companion at their destination. The similarity between this and witch stories from other regions is all too plain.

Somewhat different from other forms of witchcraft is that of werewolves or lycanthropes, well known in Europe in medieval times in France and Germany. A werewolf was a male witch who could turn himself into a gigantic wolf and roam the countryside, attacking people and killing them. The superstition was transferred to Canada during the French occupation of that country, where a werewolf was known by French-Canadians as a *loup-garou*. How the superstition turned up in New Mexico is not known, but there is a legend of a violinist who was bewitched by a woman and became a werewolf. Since he was now a witch, during his noctural wanderings he would visit witches' meetings, turn himself back into a man and play the violin for their mystic dances.

In time this man seems to have lost his power of becoming a werewolf, but not of becoming a witch. One night he and his wife went to a dance, leaving their two young daughters, Aurora and Piedad, alone—with the house lights on so the girls would not be frightened if they woke. The girls were aroused by a noise outside the house. They crept to a window and saw horrible people with red faces, and were so terrified they could not cry out.

When the husband and wife returned, they found Aurora and Piedad trembling without control, their power of speech gone. They could only point to the window and cry.

This condition continued for some time until the mother took the girls to a female witch doctor, who was able to cure Piedad, but could do nothing for Aurora, who still trembled

146

constantly, could not walk or control her body and even had to be fed.

Aurora's brothers, who either were not living at home or were away themselves on the night the strange occurrence took place, were convinced there were witches about in one of their favorite guises—owls. According to New Mexican witchcraft belief, somewhat similar to that of the silver bullet, if a witch in this form could be shot with a bullet marked with a cross, her power would be broken. The brothers marked crosses on all their bullets, loaded their guns and went out night after night in search of owls, but they never found any. And finally Aurora died. Most people believed that the father had put the curse on his daughters which had killed Aurora.

There are many other stories of witchcraft in New Mexico, but the question that occurs about all of them is the same: did they really happen? Did the supposed werewolf really turn into a wolf, and did he also bewitch his own daughters? Was the story told by the sheepherder Lujan true? What about the frightful orgy the young man witnessed by concealing himself under the buggy? Did the supposed witch Chata actually turn herself into a leaping ball of fire, and did some mysterious force chain her inside the circle drawn in the road?

There is no good proof that any of the New Mexico stories are true. They are legends that have grown up in the folklore of the state, and most of them are of doubtful veracity. Yet there are possible explanations for some of them.

There are at least two possible causes for the mysterious fireballs people were supposed to have seen in New Mexico. This is one of the regions where showers of meteorites sometimes strike the earth—the blazing pieces of rock that come out of orbit in outer space and escape being completely consumed by the intense heat generated when they enter the earth's atmosphere, traveling at thousands of miles an hour. But meteorites ordinarily embed themselves in the earth and cool off rather than leap ablaze over the desert; some very large ones have dug immense craters where they have landed. Meteorites do not seem to be a logical explanation.

Were they, then, fireballs of lightning? Many such fireballs have been seen. But in most of New Mexico there are seldom thunderstorms or rain. This, too, does not seem a satisfactory explanation for the mysterious balls of fire.

As for the supposed werewolf, it is well established that there were and perhaps still are members of a West African cult known as the leopard men, who were supposed to turn themselves into leopards, hunt down people and kill them. Some of the leopard men have been captured and found to be dressed in leopard skins with steel claws attached to the paws. The "werewolf" might have dressed himself in a wolf's skin; then it would have been easy for him to change back into a man and play at the witches' meetings. In the case of his "bewitched" daughters, the father, working a witch's evil spell, might have arranged the whole thing to scare the girls to death—and with one of them was said to have been successful. Fright, especially when there is no earthly explanation for it, can do terrible things to nervous, superstitious people.

In the case of the man and his wife who bewitched each other, both are supposed to have known a curse had been placed on them; thus it could have been the husband's and wife's own belief in the power of witchcraft that resulted in their deaths.

The supposed witch of Tajique may have believed herself a witch, but the evidence at her trial was so unbelievable to a judge who was evidently not superstitious that she escaped punishment. The testimony given against her may have been due to jealousy or hatred on the part of the sick woman's friend.

The power of the evil eye is so widely believed that there may be truth in it, but again it is a curse in which the victim knows he has been "bewitched" and he probably suffers because of his own belief that he will.

The story of the young man who followed his relatives to a witches' orgy is harder to explain. Like so many of these witch stories, it is a folklore legend that may never have happened. There is also the possibility that the young man saw the orgy in a dream or while under the influence of some drug or herb affecting the mind—possibly a large amount of marijuana, which is grown in great quantities in nearby Mexico. Or the young man may have been insane. It is very doubtful that this story is true.

Again, it must be remembered that the people of the region were mostly uneducated, credulous and very superstitious and so were apt to accept witch stories as the truth. Yet at least in some of the stories witchcraft may have been at work—not because the "witches" had magical powers, but because they were able to make their victims believe they did.

✤ ✤ ✤ 12
INDIAN WITCHCRAFT

There is always a connection between witchcraft and religion. The American Indians had a belief in a supreme being called by a number of titles, among them the Great Spirit, Manitou, Glooscap, Master of Life, Giver of Birth and Earthmaker. Opposing this doer of good was witchcraft, something that was evil and to be destroyed.

The Indians' belief in witchcraft should not be confused with their belief in medicine men, who tried to cure disease. True, medicine men had their weird methods and rituals, but they were not ordinarily considered to be witches or sorcerers. However, some Indian tribes believed that a medicine man could become a witch if he decided to use his knowledge to make someone sick instead of well.

In eastern America, the merciless attitude of the Indians toward witchcraft was especially evident in the powerful Iroquois Confederation. The Confederation was originally composed of five tribes living in what is now the state of New York—the Mohawks, Onondagas, Oneidas, Cayugas and Senecas. Early in the eighteenth century the Tuscaroras joined them, moving from the Carolinas into northern Pennsylvania and New York to make the Confederation the Six Nations.

Among the Iroquois it often took only suspicion or an accusation to cause members of these tribes to be executed without a trial for witchcraft. There are records of some executions of suspected witches. As late as 1803, four Onondaga women were accused of witchcraft. One confessed she was a witch; they took her to the top of a hill, killed her with an ax and buried her among the rocks of the summit. Two others who refused to admit their guilt were executed anyway. A fourth was spared when she admitted her guilt but promised to reform and never have anything to do with witchcraft again.

Since the Six Nations fought against the Americans in the Revolution, many of these Indians were transferred to reservations in British Canada when the war ended. During the nineteenth century an Iroquois on one of the Canadian reservations became convinced that an old Indian there was a witch. He lay in ambush as the supposed sorcerer came along and shot the old man dead. Nothing was done by the chiefs to punish the murderer, and when some of the dead man's friends were asked what they might do to avenge their companion, one replied, "Nothing. He was at that business long enough."

When the Nanticoke tribe of Pennsylvania migrated north into Iroquois territory in New York about the middle of the eighteenth century, they are said to have brought to the Onondagas a kind of witchcraft new to the Six Nations. A society of witches met secretly at night, and no member dared tell what went on there. However, rumors got about that some members turned themselves into foxes and wolves

151

at the meetings and would then run at great speed with lights flashing about them. Others assumed the form of turkeys or huge owls that flew very fast from one village to another, blowing worms or hair into people—one of the ways in which the white men's witchcraft was supposed to have the power of killing its victims.

The witches could avoid discovery by turning themselves into a stone or a log. Nevertheless, the Onondagas took action against this evil society. They accused fifty suspected members and burned them all to death.

The Onondagas had an elaborate method of driving away evil spirits and curing sick people believed to be bewitched. An organization known as the False Faces held secret meetings. When its members appeared in public to cure a supposedly bewitched person, they all wore large wooden masks, carved and painted in grotesque designs, with eyeholes decorated with brass or tin, and long, flowing wigs of horsehair.

One woman was associated with the False Faces and knew their names. She was called Go-go-sa Ho-nun-na-tase-ta, or Keeper of the False Faces. She took care of the masks and other regalia.

Indians loved feasts and one was always a part of the ceremony when a sick person believed to be bewitched was to be cured by having the evil spirits drawn out of him. The feast was prepared at the sick person's home.

The False Faces, masked and led by the female Keeper of the False Faces, would come into the house in single file. In addition to the mask, each one wore a tattered blanket and carried a rattle made from a turtle shell. They stirred the ashes on the hearth, and each in turn sprinkled some over the patient's head and hair. This was supposed to drive out the evil spirits harming the afflicted person. The False Faces then performed their special dance, using their rattles, and left, each taking his portion of the feast, to be eaten when he reached home.

The False Faces were actually performing a kind of witchcraft in place of the medicine man, who cured by means of his own special herbs, roots and other remedies, but it was a benevolent kind of witchcraft designed to combat the evil form.

To combat evil spirits, tribes of the Algonquin family, of which the Iroquois were a part, used several methods. The principal one was an appeal to the Great Spirit. The Indians used and prized tobacco long before the white men came to America. They believed it was a gift from the Great Spirit, who was also fond of it. Thus, in order to gain his favor, especially for a good crop season or if disease or some other ill fortune had befallen them, they would make offerings of tobacco at ceremonies held for the purpose.

Another way of ensuring good crops or obtaining relief from trouble was through the use of clan bundles. Clan bundles contained the skins, claws and beaks of animals and birds. When a ceremony was held—and it was a practice always to have one at planting and harvesting time—the bundle was opened by the bundle keeper, a position of high honor which descended like a royal crown from one member to another of a single family. The other members of the clan (a clan was a smaller unit than a tribe, composed of the inhabitants of one of the long houses used as dwellings by the Iroquois in place of wigwams) would be summoned to the bundle keeper's lodgings for a feast at which the main course was a sacred white dog, for the Indians were fond of roast dog. The clansmen would sit by the opened bundle, stuff themselves with food, make offerings of tobacco to the Great Spirit and sing songs. Clan bundles were also used by Algonquin tribes in the vicinity of the Great Lakes.

The Creeks, one of the five once-powerful nations in the Southeast (the Five Civilized Tribes, consisting of the Choctaws, Chickasaws, Cherokees, Seminoles and the Upper and Lower Creeks), used bundles. Since these were taken into battle to bring victory, they were known as war bundles, carried on the back of the war ceremonialist and never allowed to touch the ground, an event which would cause a defeat. Somewhat similar, far to the west, was the sacred white buffalo hide, carried by a woman during buffalo hunts by the Omaha tribe.

In the Southwest, Indian witchcraft, practiced into modern times, possibly even today to some extent, was different in some ways and similar in others to the beliefs of the eastern Indians. In Arizona the Apache had their medicine men, but they also had witches, especially sorcerers and love witches.

The sorcerers were considered the most dangerous of witches and were the most feared. Both men and women could be sorcerers, but male ones were more common. In order to become a sorcerer, an Apache had to go to an already established one and undergo an extensive training course before he was qualified to practice sorcery.

Love witches were less common than sorcerers and their role was to aid romance through spells. It was believed that a love witch could put a spell on a woman that would make her pursue the man who desired her wherever he wished. Again, this was similar to some forms of white witchcraft already described. However, there was a connection between love witches and sorcerers. Either could learn and practice the magic arts of the other and the two types were supposed to meet secretly at night and hold witch dances from dusk to dawn.

There was a distinct difference in the way medicine men and witches worked, according to the Apache belief. Medicine men used their power openly at public ceremonies and controlled it through chants. In their rituals they often used sand paintings, in which clean sand is spread on the floor of a dwelling, or hogan as it is called. On the white sand pictures were drawn by sprinkling on red, yellow and black dry colors, usually in the image of an Indian god. And the medicine men's power was used only for good in diagnosing and curing illness.

On the other hand, sorcerers used their power only in secret. They worked their magic by other means than chants. They did not use sand paintings. And their power was used for evil instead of good, to cause illness, death or sometimes insanity.

Sorcerers used their enchantments by casting spells on their victims, poisoning them or injecting some object into the person's body. Enchantment by spell was a complex operation. It could be accomplished by making a threat of harm to the victim or simply by thinking malicious thoughts about him. It was not necessary for the sorcerer to meet him face to face. The spell itself was repeated four times and sometimes had a line from a ceremonial chant, but it was said backwards.

The power of a spell varied according to how it was cast. One way of increasing the effect was to walk around the victim four times or to circle his house four times. Sometimes the sorcerer placed four pieces of wood on the north, east, south and west sides of the house. Or he might bury a piece of wood or small stone near the house or at some place where the victim went to drink or take his ease, as happened in the case of the false Georgia cunjer doctor already described. Spells could also be used against cattle and other livestock, as well as crops. They could be cast to counteract the curing effect of a medicine man's ceremonies.

Sorcerers who used poison always carried it with them, hidden under their clothing in a buckskin pouch. It might be snake or scorpion poison or even that of the bee; people strongly allergic to bee stings have been killed by a single sting, so a large dose would be dangerous to anyone.

There was also sorcerer's poison that could be used only by male sorcerers. It contained a variety of ingredients, including the powdered skin of human corpses, powdered rattlesnake skin and bits of wood from trees struck by lightning. The poison was usually injected into the victim's body by putting it into his food or dropping it into his mouth or nostrils while he was sleeping.

Apache, who dreaded sorcery greatly, used turquoise beads as one form of protection; others were cattail pollen and the breast feathers of an eagle. A case is described in Apache witchcraft in which an old man always carried with him a bean he believed would instantly crack open if a sorcerer's magic threatened him. An Apache who believed he was bewitched might seek out a sorcerer whose powers he thought were greater than those of the one who had put the spell upon him.

The Apache usually brought suspected witches to trial. First the accused one would be summoned before the headmen of his village and accused. If he denied the charge, he was strung up by his wrists to the limb of a tree with his toes barely touching the ground. If he still refused to admit his guilt, a fire might be lighted under him while he was relentlessly questioned and his belongings searched for poison.

Although the mockery of such "trials" is believed to be used no longer, there is a report of a witchcraft trial held during the 1950s by the Apache. The suspected witch was placed in the center of a circle of his neighbors, warned he would be shot if he tried to escape and left with nothing to eat or drink until he confessed.

A person found guilty of witchcraft at an Apache trial was not given a sentence; he was simply feared and avoided afterward. The convicted witch had a lonely life. Among the Zunis, a branch of the Hopi tribe, one who confessed to witchcraft might be exiled if he confessed, but if he did not he was tortured or might be hanged.

The Navahos, neighbors of the Apache in Arizona and New Mexico and the largest group of present-day American Indians, have always had a strong belief in witchcraft. Both men and women became witches, but there were more male ones, and most of the female witches were old women.

Some took up witchcraft to make money. Since Navaho witchcraft has a close relationship with death and the dead, and corpses were in demand, some made money by robbing graves. Another money-making method required the cooperation of two witches. Usually the victim was rich and could afford to pay well to have a curse lifted from him. So one of the partners would put a spell on the victim, who fell ill, doubtless because the witch casting the spell saw to it that his prey knew he was bewitched. Then the confederate witch would come to the man and offer to lift the spell for a high price. The two witches then split the profit from this abominable scheme. When profit was not the object, a person might turn to witchcraft to harm an enemy. As was the case with some other tribes, in order to become a witch a Navaho had to first kill a close relative, usually a brother or sister.

Navaho belief in witches' practices is much like that of other tribes. The witches roamed at night in the form of wolves, coyotes, bears, foxes, owls or crows and traveled at great speed. When dust fell from the smokehole of a Navaho hogan (the familiar tripod-shaped dwelling used by western Indians), loud noises were heard at night or other unusual commotions took place, a witch was believed to have been there.

Navaho witches also had their secret meetings or witches' Sabbaths. These were held to initiate new members or to kill victims at a distance. The meetings generally took place in a cave, with all members masked and naked, their bodies painted with mystic symbols. They sat in a circle around baskets filled with the flesh of corpses stolen from graves, which they often ate. A "chief witch" directed the ceremonies.

Navahos also had their sorcerers. The sorcerer obtained hair, nails, excretions or body dirt of his prey or, if that was impossible, a bit of his clothing. These things were burned with flesh taken from a corpse in a grave, or under a tree that had been struck by lightning. The sorcerer recited a spell. To "pray a person under the ground," the sorcerer invoked his spell in turn against all parts of the victim's body, beginning with the top of the head.

Another way of putting a spell on someone was to open the body of a toad which had been burned, put a charm inside it and recite the spell. Or a sorcerer might whisper a spell when close to his victim. Also, as is the case with many other forms of witchcraft, the sorcerer might make a clay image of his victim or carve it of wood and then stick a sharp-pointed instrument into it.

Navaho sorcery was also used against animals, grain, crops and other property. If a blight of grasshoppers, caterpillars or other pests appeared to destroy crops, the Navahos ascribed it to sorcery.

With the Indians of the Northwest, the medicine man was a witchcraft figure, known as a shaman, a name used by tribes in other parts of America. He was an important and powerful figure, supposed to have wonderful powers indeed. He could kill people by witchcraft, keep possession of their souls and use them as his slaves. He was a healer like other medicine men, but like many sorcerers he considered that disease was caused by a stick, worm or some other object that had gotten into the sick person's body. In order for a cure to be obtained, the object had to be removed.

First, in order to diagnose the disease, the shaman had to "see" it and thus determine where the object to be removed was located. For this purpose he peered through a quartz crystal to let him view whatever was troubling the sick person. If the shaman realized that the illness could not be cured, he would say that it had been caused by another medicine man whose power was greater than his own. If he was not sure he could bring about a cure, he might call in a special worker of magic, a convenient way of shifting the blame if the patient died.

However, if the shaman decided he could cure the patient, he would sing to the accompaniment of a rattle. In the case of a sick hunter, the shaman would use a bunch of deer hoofs in place of the rattle; for a farmer, a gourd with pebbles inside it.

For several nights the shaman would blow on the patient or wave feathers over him and then smoke a pipe. At last he would approach the sick person and suck on the part of his body where the object causing the trouble was supposed to be, or use a cupping device whose suction would accomplish the same result. Suddenly he would display the object in his hand to those gathered at the patient's bedside; it would then be destroyed or thrown away. The patient was then supposed to recover; in truth, if the illness was not a fatal one, he should have been on the road to recovery after all that time, anyhow. And of course the shaman had his alibi of some superior power to his own if a cure did not result.

Almost all Indian tribes had taboos. At their ceremonies there would always be some object so sacred that it could not be touched. If anyone was foolish enough to do so, the result would be fatal to him.

Where did Indian witchcraft originate, and why does it have similarities to other kinds of witchcraft? Since witchcraft goes back to the earliest recorded times, and since ethnologists are quite well agreed that the first discoverers of America came from Siberia across the narrow Bering Strait, they doubtless brought witchcraft with them. These Siberian people are believed to have settled in the Northwest and then gradually began a great migration which distributed these ancient Indians throughout what is now the United States and Canada. However, in the Southwest, much of the Indian witchcraft belief doubtless came from Mexico.

It would require many more pages to describe in detail

all the forms of witchcraft and sorcery used by the Indian nations and tribes throughout America, yet there were many similarities in them. This will at least give a good idea of the powerful hold that witchcraft had, and in some cases still has, on American Indians.

There are scores of tales about witchcraft that are supposed to have happened in bygone times among the eastern Indian tribes of America. Most are fantastic, though they were believed by the tribes in which they originated because the existence of witchcraft was almost universally accepted among red men everywhere. They do not seem any less believable than evidence accepted at white witchcraft trials, especially during the Salem witchcraft delusion.

Perhaps the most credible of these legends is supposed to have happened in New Hampshire, where several such weird occurrences are said to have taken place among the white settlers. The story of Chocorua affected the white men, but its witchcraft, if that is what it was, came as a result of an Indian curse or spell.

The White Mountains of New Hampshire, where the legend is centered, are not only beautiful, but spectacular for their rocky grandeur, attracting thousands of tourists to the area. In the Presidential Range, four peaks named for early Presidents of the United States thrust themselves skyward, one after the other, all over 5,000 feet high, with Mt. Washington, over 6,000 feet, the highest in the northeastern United States. But one mountain, some twenty miles to the south and only about 3,500 feet high, stands almost alone. It is unique, not only for its bald, jagged peak, but because there is something haunting and mysterious about this lonely mountain. It is called Chocorua, named for an Indian medicine man of great influence among his people, who was believed by early settlers to be endowed with the powers of darkness.

The Indians of Chocorua's tribe were friendly people of the Abenaki nation. Like some of the other New England tribes, their friendship was sometimes annoying, since they would often come to visit the white settlements in large numbers, expecting to be welcomed, fed and entertained as long as they wished to stay. But considering that they were so amiable and never made war or raided the settlements, such inconveniences were small indeed.

Chocorua was entirely different from the others, however. Although uneducated, he had a keen intelligence that unfortunately sometimes made him give way to ferocious passions. This was plain to the white men by his haughty bearing and his black, piercing eyes that could not conceal a smoldering hatred for the whites. As time passed, however, and Chocorua made no hostile move, their fear of him subsided and even the children were not afraid of him.

Chocorua had a son about ten years old. Caroline Campbell, wife of Cornelius Campbell, took a fancy to the Indian boy, giving him presents of mirrors, colored beads and so on. Like all boys of his age, the young Indian was inquisitive, and when he came to the Campbell house he would poke about, investigating the utensils, tools and other things of which the red men had known nothing till the settlers came.

The settlement was having trouble with a fox which was forever raiding the henyards. The Campbells decided to be rid of the animal and prepared a bottle of poison in which they could soak some meat, leaving it where the fox would

162

find it. But Chocorua's son, rummaging about the Campbell house one day, came upon the bottle of poison and drank it. The Campbells knew nothing of what he had done, but when the boy reached home he died in agony.

Chocorua was sure his beloved son had been deliberately poisoned. He plotted a terrible revenge. One June morning, Cornelius Campbell left his cabin to work as usual in the fields. At noon he went home to dinner. He ate no dinner prepared by his wife. She and all his children lay dead in the cabin, their bodies frightfully mangled by Chocorua's tomahawk.

Cornelius Campbell was so stricken by the catastrophe that for days he was like a man bereft of his senses. Indeed, many of the settlers feared he would never regain his reason. But at last he recovered enough to plan vengeance upon Chocorua, who had fled into hiding. He would hunt down the medicine man and kill him.

The other Indians were away on a hunting expedition when Chocorua committed his hideous crime, and they had not yet returned. Mr. Campbell and other settlers, searching the wilderness, finally saw Chocorua. He had climbed the mountain and his familiar, powerful figure was recognized on the ledges of the summit, peering out into the distance. He was apparently looking for the returning hunting party, confident that they would support him against the whites. Chocorua was seen there several times, so it was apparent that he was hiding somewhere on the mountain. It was surrounded by a party led by Campbell, and the searchers began to close in.

Then, when the murderer was seen again on the summit, Cornelius Campbell climbed after him. Approaching the top, he called out, ordering the Indian to throw himself off into a deep abyss just below.

Chocorua replied calmly, "The Great Spirit gave life to Chocorua, and Chocorua will not throw it away at the command of a white man."

Cornelius Campbell raised his musket, took careful aim and fired. The bullet struck Chocorua in the neck. For a moment he tottered on the brink of the precipice, but he recovered long enough to shout: "A curse upon ye, white men! May the Great Spirit curse ye when he speaks in the clouds, and his words are fire! Chocorua had a son and ye killed him while the sky looked bright! Lightning blast your crops! Wind and fire destroy your dwellings! The Evil Spirit breathe death upon your cattle! Your graves lie in the warpath of the Indians! Panthers howl and wolves fatten upon your bones! Chocorua goes to the Great Spirit—his curse stays with the white men!"

Then Chocorua sank to the ground and died. The settlers left the body there on the rocky mountain which today bears his name, until only his bones, whitened by the sun, remained.

Chocorua's curse came to pass. His tribe took up their tomahawks and scalping knives against the settlers. Violent storms tore up trees, which fell on the cabins. The people's crops failed and their cattle died. An epidemic of sickness spread through the settlement and many died. And at last those who had survived moved away. During that period Cornelius Campbell, who had become a hermit, was found dead in his hut.

Later on a new settlement was established at the base of Mt. Chocorua. But these settlers' cattle were afflicted with a strange disease that killed many of them. It was some years before the mystery was solved; the water in some springs where the cattle drank had become polluted with chloride of lime which seeped in from a deposit on the mountain.

Yet the questions persisted: Had it been Chocorua's curse that had put an end to the original settlement? And had it now showed itself again in the deaths of the cattle in the new settlement? Chocorua, the medicine man or witch doctor, had called upon both the Great Spirit and the Evil Spirit in his curse. What happened sounds more like the work of the Evil Spirit, Satan, than the benevolent Great Spirit of the Indians. Or did it all happen simply by chance?

Farther west, in what is now the state of New York, the intense hatred of witchcraft among the Iroquois is illustrated by an Onondaga legend about a young Indian man who joined a coven of witches in order to expose and destroy them.

The young warrior suspected that witches of the tribe were responsible for the serious illness of his brother. Believing that a certain old woman was a witch, he went to her and said he wanted to become one.

In accordance with the general practice of Indian witchcraft requiring that a prospective new member must do evil to someone close to him, the old woman said, "If you are very much in earnest you may become a witch, but you must first go to your sister and point at her. Then she will be taken sick and after a time will die."

When the young man agreed, the old woman said that when he had done so she would take him to the witches' meeting place. He went home and told his sister the whole

165

story. They decided on a plan: she would pretend to be ill and let it be known so that the witches would suspect no treachery.

That night the young Onondaga brave went to the old woman's house and told her he had done what she had ordered him to do. They then started for the witches' meeting place. Whenever he could do so without her noticing, he broke off a twig so that there would be a trail leading to the secret meeting place.

Suddenly he was startled when the old woman sprang into a tree. As he looked up in the darkness he saw, not a woman, but a great panther with sharp teeth and claws, spitting and snarling at him. The young man was terrified, but he managed to control his fear and pretend he was not disturbed.

With that, the old woman changed back to her natural form and came down. "Didn't I frighten you?" she demanded.

"Oh, no," he replied. "I was not afraid. I would like to be like that myself."

They went on and came to an open space in the woods, crowded with old men and women and a few young women. A fire was burning in the center over which hung a tiny kettle. Above it hung a bunch of snakes from which blood was dripping into the kettle. When it was full of blood, all the witches took a sip of it. The young man pretended to do so. Meanwhile, he was looking around so he would be able to identify those who had come to the meeting.

The witches then turned into the shapes of many animals, birds and reptiles. They gave him an owl's head and told him to put it on over his own. As soon as he did so he lost all control of himself and flew away, screeching like an owl.

He lit on the roof of his house, took off the owl's head, was himself again and climbed down.

He went into the house and pointed, not at his sister, but at the dog. The next day the dog was ill and soon died. Meanwhile, the sister pretended she was sick, and as the news spread through the village many of the witches who had been at the meeting came to visit the supposedly ailing young woman to express their sympathy and the hope that she would soon be well again.

The young man now had the evidence he needed. He got his warrior friends together and told them what had happened. That night, well armed, they all started out, following the trail of broken twigs the young man had left.

When they reached the clearing in the woods, a meeting was going on. They crept stealthily up to watch the proceedings. A speaker was addressing the witches, telling them they would go to heaven and be rewarded by the Great Spirit for killing people because this would keep their victims from becoming bad or having ill fortune.

At a signal from the young warrior, his companions rushed in with him and, following the Indian practice of destroying all witches, killed every one of them.

All this might be believable but for the fantastic parts about how the old woman turned herself into a panther and of how the young warrior was changed into an owl. Yet although the story is doubtless pure legend, there is the possibility that the old woman put the young Onondaga into a trance in which she appeared to him as a panther, and that although he was at the witches' meeting, what he saw and how he was changed into an owl might have been illusions of his trance that ended when he reached home.

With the possible exception of that about Chocorua, practically all the scores of American Indian witchcraft stories are fanciful. Yet in their way they are no more incredible than most white witchcraft tales. They concern the supernatural, and there are just as many incredible supernatural stories the world over.

❖ ❖ ❖ 13
TODAY'S WITCHCRAFT

Witchcraft beliefs have always flourished among superstitious, ignorant people and often among learned men and women. One might think that with the great advances in education in the United States, witchcraft in this country, as well as others, would at least be critically ill if not completely dead. Far from it. Witchcraft beliefs are present in the United States today on a scale never before equaled, although of course there are far more people now than in colonial days, and it is also true that a great many people today have no belief at all in witchcraft, while in colonial America almost everyone believed in it in one way or another.

No one knows how many covens of witches exist in the United States today. There is limited information about a good many, but witchcraft has always been a secret practice, and most of those who now call themselves witches tell little of their doings, especially if they are designed to work evil. Those who openly declare themselves to be witches are generally "white witches," who profess to do only good with their witchcraft.

169

Probably the most famous of all white witches today is Sybil Leek. She was born in England and learned her witchcraft from her grandmother, one of a line of professional witches going back to the twelfth century. Sybil Leek became a healer. She uses her expert knowledge of herbs and other natural medicinal preparations, as well as charms. The powers she appears to have, however, come from psychic healing, a combination of psychology and philosophy, as well as from extreme concentration on what she wishes to accomplish, learned in her days of training to be a witch.

In England, Sybil Leek gained a wide reputation for her success in curing illnesses, some of which doctors considered hopeless. Finally she came to the United States. Her fame had preceded her, and she was overwhelmed by people seeking her aid. She is now a permanent resident of America, has written books on witchcraft and is also expert on astrology—an area closely allied in some ways with witchcraft, especially in predicting the future. If all modern witchcraft were like that practiced by Sybil Leek, who considers it a religion, it would be a widely respected profession.

There are many other witches' covens all over the United States. One example is the coven on Long Island organized by Dr. Raymond Buckland, its high priest, a thoroughly educated man who has a doctorate in anthropology. He is assisted by his wife, who is the high priestess of the cult. They too consider witchcraft a religion.

The cult meets once a week in a special room in the Buckland home. Little is revealed of what takes place except that the ritual is performed by candlelight and the witches dance naked to weird music. Yet anyone hoping to take part in a wild orgy at which alcohol or drugs are used is doomed to disappointment, according to Dr. Buckland. Nothing of the sort is allowed, and those who apply for membership in the coven are carefully investigated.

Dr. Buckland says supernatural energy that can perform healing magic flows from the witches' bodies. In the dances the witches' energies are combined, and also flow more freely with clothing removed. Dr. Buckland tells of a person paralyzed from the waist down who was made to walk again at a special ritual in which all the witches' energies were concentrated on achieving the cure. Dr. Buckland lectures on witchcraft at colleges throughout the country and also operates the Buckland Museum of Witchcraft and Magick in Bay Shore, Long Island, which contains exhibits pertaining to many forms of witchcraft collected by him on visits to Europe, some of the items ancient and rare.

Also on Long Island, in 1973 a young high school senior who calls herself Nikki, and at that time claimed to have practiced witchcraft for ten years, presented a lecture at a local library. She had her own coven of thirteen witches and used charms to work spells, though only for good. Like Sybil Leek, Nikki used intense concentration in her work and called her witchcraft a religion. She claimed that with the aid of her coven a woman was cured of cancer.

These are but two of the many witches' covens all over the country today. The subject is so popular that a number of colleges have offered courses in it.

Unfortunately, there are organizations composed of "black witches" devoted solely to doing evil. The largest one known was said to have 5,000 members in 1970 and was growing rapidly. It was begun chiefly as an amusement for the members, but its reputation has become very evil. The creed is that the seven deadly sins—anger, covetousness, envy, gluttony, lust, pride and laziness—are virtues and should be practiced as much as possible.

This cult's headquarters, located in San Francisco, are in a house painted black outside and in. The place contains a skeleton, human skulls for candleholders and other grisly items. Black masses are performed there in which the service resembles that of a Christian church, but with everything reversed to idolize Satan and mock God. The chapel and the candles are black. A cross is hung upside down on the altar; the chants that replace hymns blaspheme God and exalt Satan. The head of the cult calls himself "high priest of the Devil, Satan, Lucifer, Beelzebub or any other evil name you can think of."

There are other covens. One, in Toledo, Ohio, is a cult that worships Satan and considers him the "blessed savior." Another calls itself the Women's International Terrorist Conspiracy from Hell (WITCH).

African and West Indian forms of witchcraft, including voodoo and obeah, still abound, especially in cities having a large Black or Hispanic population. In the ghetto districts of New York City, for example, dozens of little shops stock materials for these types of witchcraft. Some, following the modern do-it-yourself practice, sell complete witch kits. Graveyard dust is available, as well as candles that are supposed to produce spells and are known as DUME (Death Unto Mine Enemy), bats' blood, the familiar dolls—including pins, to cast spells—and charms of all kinds.

Persecution of suspected witches still goes on occasionally. A horse trainer at a track in West Virginia moved into a quiet neighborhood in a nearby town with his family in the late 1960s. The neighbors looked down on him because he worked at the racetrack.

He was an intelligent fellow and became interested in parapsychology, the study of supernatural happenings. The news of it got about and the neighbors' dislike turned to hatred and suspicion. One of them, the horse trainer claimed, nailed a large wooden cross to a tree next door. Another was said to have crossed himself every time he passed the suspected witch, who himself was also a devoted Catholic. In July, 1968, the trainer claimed that he was attacked and beaten in an alley.

At last the persecuted man filed a suit for defamation of character against ten of his neighbors, alleging they had called him a Devil worshipper having close connections with Satan. One witness against him said the trainer took her and two friends to a cemetery and performed a black mass. The witness claimed the man had put a wine bottle on a tombstone. It fell off, but was miraculously restored to its place by some unknown force.

The horse trainer admitted he had performed the ceremony, evidently out of desperation, for he insisted it was to show the three women that witchcraft was "a lot of nothing, that it was trickery, that he had no powers," but the women ran away.

The suit never came to trial. The ten neighbors evidently decided that they might find themselves in trouble that could cost them a good deal of money in damages. They apologized to the trainer, who was decent enough to accept, drop the suit and live in peace thereafter.

One of three witchcraft-related cases of the twentieth century in Pennsylvania, in 1906, also never came to trial. A farmer in the Mahanoy valley had trouble with his livestock. For thirteen months his horses, cows and swine continued to fall ill of a mysterious disease and die. The farmer could not understand it, since his stables were clean, the animals were provided good food and the water was pure. A veterinarian was unable to stop the strange ailment. Finally, the farmer accused a woman in the neighborhood of witchcraft and of putting a spell on his livestock. But instead of having her arrested, perhaps because he felt no modern jury would convict her, he paid her a large sum of money to lift the curse. Apparently she did, for he had no more trouble.

The most sensational modern witchcraft-related trial, unbelievable as it may seem, was held in Reading, Pennsylvania, in 1929. John Blymer was tried for the murder of Nelson D. Rehmeyer in a farmhouse in a lonely section of York County.

"I did not kill him," Blymer first insisted at the trial.

"Why did you go to Rehmeyer's house, then, if not to kill him?" the prosecutor demanded.

"I went to get a lock of hair or a book called *Long Lost Friend*."

The prosecutor asked what he wanted with such things.

"To break a spell that Rehmeyer had put on me. . . ."

"When you killed him, did that break the spell?"

In his reply, Blymer seems to have forgotten his plea of innocence. He answered, "Yes."

"Did you feel better?"

"Yes. Now I can eat and sleep and rest better and I am not pining away."

The jury found him guilty and although Pennsylvania then had the death penalty, life imprisonment was recommended. There is little doubt that he was insane, for he had

174

escaped from an insane asylum in 1921 only forty-eight hours after being placed there. One reason that the trial was so sensational was that there were those in the region where Rehmeyer lived who believed he actually was a witch doctor.

Later, in 1934, Albert Shimsky, who lived near Pottsville, Pennsylvania, was tried for murdering a Mrs. Mummey. Shimsky claimed he was justified because the woman was a witch and the Bible commands: "Thou shalt not suffer a witch to live." While Shimsky was in jail awaiting trial, a psychologist examined him and reported that he was "a mental and emotional infant." They sent Shimsky away to an insane asylum.

The story of Lithobolia, the Stone-Throwing Demon, and the strange showers of stones near the house of the famous Dr. John of New Orleans had a counterpart in the twentieth century. It is just as incredible, is even more fully substantiated and has never been solved.

In February of 1958 in the home of Mr. and Mrs. James M. Herrmann in Seaford, a Long Island suburb, on a quiet residential street, pandemonium broke loose. For several weeks bottles jumped about and their screwed-on tops popped off. Objects flew through the air. A statue of the Virgin Mary, eighteen inches high, flew off a table and landed twelve feet away. A phonograph sailed across a room. A heavy bookcase toppled over.

The police were called and detectives investigated; one was present when an object flew from its place. Learned students of the mystic arts came to the house and offered their opinions on the mystery. Newspapers and other news media spread the story far and wide. Traffic jams developed as "rubberneckers" tried to get a look at the house.

During March the strange happenings ceased abruptly

and did not recur, but no one has ever satisfactorily explained the case of the flying objects. Things that smack of witchcraft still do happen.

Indeed, another case, similar in some respects, but far worse, took place in 1949. A young boy living near Washington, D.C. became possessed by some apparently supernatural influence. So fully supported by evidence and witnesses was this case that although the boy was not a Catholic, this church became interested and apparently was successful in what doctors and psychiatrists failed to do.

The boy began to speak in a different voice and language from his own, and to vomit strange-smelling fluids. When an aunt visited him and sat down on his bed, she was thrown against the wall. The boy was in great pain and when the aunt suddenly heard a slap there was the imprint of a human hand across his face.

Exorcism, the supposed power of driving evil spirits out of a possessed person, is a part of the Catholic ritual. A priest was sent to see the boy and spent the night in his room. The good father had a bad time of it. A mat on which he was lying slid all over the floor. The furniture moved in and tried to assault him. A bottle fell from its place on the wall to the tile floor, but did not break.

The Catholic Church decided to exorcise the boy, who had been moved from Georgetown University Hospital to a hospital in St. Louis. Doctors and nurses were present as the priest performed the ritual of exorcism. The boy had developed superhuman strength; he resisted the priest and injured his arm, but the ritual was performed and the boy recovered. Today he is perfectly normal, is married, has three children and has not the slightest remembrance of the strange things that happened to him.

A novel, *The Exorcist,* based on the occurrence, was published and the motion picture rights were sold in Hollywood. The film, greatly changed from the actual facts, was released early in 1974 and has played to large audiences. As though the strange happenings that had actually taken place were being turned against those who made the picture, the director faced endless problems in making it. An unexplained fire destroyed a house that was built as a set, and all sorts of other strange things happened. The film was over three months behind schedule when completed. The director was quoted as saying he had trouble sleeping at night and that although he had never believed in the occult, he had become convinced that there was such a thing as possession by demons.

Witchcraft has existed and has had its believers for countless centuries. Today, wise men still study and try to solve its unexplained mysteries. There is no indication that it will die out, even in our advanced civilization of the twentieth century.

SUGGESTED FURTHER
READINGS

Few of the books used as sources for research in writing this book are easily obtainable in any but the largest of libraries. Much of the material came from publications of historical and folklore societies which would be found in libraries in the various regions covered by the book, but are not likely to be available in the smaller libraries elsewhere.

Probably the best source of information about witchcraft, everywhere, is *The Encyclopedia of Witchcraft and Demonology*, by Roselle Hope Robbins. It makes fascinating reading and should be available in most good-sized libraries.

For background on the history of witchcraft, *Witchcraft in England*, by Christina Hole, goes into the origins of witchcraft as well as how it flourished in England. Another good general book on witchcraft is *A Book of Witchcraft*, by Raymond Lamont Brown.

Highly recommended for its detailed story of Louisiana

witchcraft is *Voodoo in New Orleans,* by Robert Tallant, though unfortunately it is hard to obtain.

For Indian witchcraft lore, Ruth Murray Underhill's two books, *Red Man's America* and *Red Man's Religion,* are recommended if available.

BIBLIOGRAPHY

Aurand, A. Monroe. *The "Pow-Wow" Book*. Harrisburg: Aurand Press, 1929.

Aurand, A. Monroe, Jr. *The Realness of Witchcraft in America*. Harrisburg: Aurand Press, 1942.

Barstow, George. *The History of New Hampshire*. Concord: I. S. Boyd, 1842.

Basso, Keith H. "Western Apache Witchcraft." Anthropological Papers, University of Arizona, No. 15, 1969.

Bayard, S. P. "Witchcraft Magic and Spirits on the Border of Pennsylvania and West Virginia." Journal of American Folklore, Vol. 51, 1938.

Beauchamp, William M. "Iroquois Folk Lore." Empire State Historical Publication XXXI, 1922.

Botkin, B. A. (ed.). *A Treasury of New England Folklore*. New York: Crown, 1947.

Brown, Raymond Lamont. *A Book of Witchcraft*. New York: Taplinger, 1971.

Burt, Wesley R., Jr. "Witchcraft in New Mexico." El Palacio, Vol. XLVII, April, 1940, No. 4.

Campa, Arthur L. "Superstition and Witchcraft Along the Rio Grande." The Westerners 1949 Brand Book.

Chamberlayne, Richard. "Lithobolia or the Stone-Throwing Demon." Magazine of History, Extra No. 90, Vol. 23, No. 2, 1923.

Clemens, Gurney W. "Comments on the Pennsylvania Germans in the Diary of James L. Morris." Historical Review of Berks County, Vol. XI, No. 4, July, 1946.

Cross, Tom Peete. "Witchcraft in North Carolina." University of North Carolina Studies in Philology, Vol. 16, July, 1919, No. 3.

Davis, Richard Blake. "The Devil in Virginia in the Seventeenth Century." Virginia Magazine, Vol. 65, April, 1957, No. 2.

Drake, Samuel Adams. *A Book of New England Legends and Folk Lore.* Boston: Little, Brown, 1910.

Dufour, Charles L. *Ten Flags in the Wind—the Story of Louisiana.* New York: Harper & Row, 1967.

Folsom, Joseph Fulford. "Witches in New Jersey." New Jersey Historical Society Proceedings, New Series, Vol. 7, 1922.

Fulton, J. T. "The Lights of Brown Mountain." North Carolina Folklore, June, 1948.

Grinnell, George Bird. *Blackfoot Lodge Tales.* Lincoln: University of Nebraska Press, 1962.

Gummere, Amelia Mott. *Witchcraft and Quakerism.* Philadelphia: Biddle Press, 1908.

Harden, John. *The Devil's Tramping Ground and Other North Carolina Mystery Stories.* Chapel Hill: University of North Carolina Press, 1949.

Hark, Ann. *Hex Marks the Spot.* Philadelphia: Lippincott, 1938.

Harrington, M. Raymond. "An Abenaki Witch Story." Journal of American Folk-Lore, Vol. 47, 1934.

Heinzmann, Louis J. "Are Barn Signs Hex Marks?" Historical Review of Berks County, Vol. XII, Oct. 1946, No. 1.

Hill, Ralph Nading. *Yankee Kingdom—Vermont and New Hampshire.* New York: Harper, 1960.

Hodge, Frederick Webb (ed.). *Handbook of American Indians North of Mexico.* New York: Pageant, 1959.

Hoffman, W. F. "Folk-Lore of the Pennsylvania Germans." Journal of American Folk-Lore, Vol. 1, 1888.

Hole, Christina. *Witchcraft in England.* New York: Scribner, 1947.

Hudson, Arthur Palmer, and McCarter, Peter Kyle. "The Bell Witch of Tennessee and Mississippi, a Folk Legend." Journal of American Folk-Lore, Vol. 47, 1934.

Ingram, M. V. *An Authenticated History of the Famous Bell Witch.* Nashville: Sutliff & Co., 1894.

Johnson, Guion Griffis. *Ante-Bellum North Carolina.* Chapel Hill: University of North Carolina Press, 1937.

Josephy, Alvin M. *The Indian Heritage of America.* New York: Knopf, 1971.

Kluckhorn, Clyde. "Navaho Witchcraft." Harvard University. Papers of the Peabody Museum of American Archaeology and Ethnology, Vol. 22, No. 2, 1944.

Langden, Carolyn S. "The Case of Lydia Gilbert (Witchcraft in Connecticut)." New England Galaxy, Vol. V, No. 3, Winter, 1964.

Leland, Charles G. *The Algonquin Legends of New England.* Boston: Houghton Mifflin, 1898.

Lyon, John. "Witchcraft in New York." New York Historical Society Collections, Publication Fund, 1869, Clarendon Papers.

MacCracken, Henry Noble. *Blithe Dutchess.* New York: Hastings, 1958.

Magruder, Harriet. *A History of Louisiana.* New York: D. C. Heath, 1909.

Mahr, August C. "Origin and Significance of Pennsylvania-Dutch Barn Symbols." Ohio State Archaeological and Ethnological Quarterly, Jan.-March, 1945, Vol. 54, No. 1.

May, Ralph. *Early Portsmouth History.* Boston: C. E. Goodspeed, 1926.

Murray, Margaret Alice. *The Witch Cult in Western Europe.* Oxford: Clarendon Press, 1921.

Neifert, William W. "Witchcraft." The Pennsylvania-German, Vol. IX, March, 1908, No. 3.

Nelson, William (ed.). *Archives of the State of New Jersey.* Newark: Daily Advertiser Printing House, 1888.

Notestein, Wallace. *A History of Witchcraft in England from 1558 to 1718.* New York: Russell & Russell, 1965.

Overton, Marion F. "Long Island Witchcraft." Long Island Forum, Vol. 14, Oct. 1951, No. 10.

Padilla, Floy. "Witch Stories from Tapia Azul and Tres Fulgores." New Mexico Folklore Record, Vol. 6, 1951-52.

Parke, Francis Neale. "Witchcraft in Maryland." Maryland Historical Magazine, Vol. XXXI, Dec. 1936, No. 4.

Parrinder, Geoffrey. *Witchcraft: European and African.* London: Faber & Faber, 1963.

Robbins, Roselle Hope. *The Encyclopedia of Witchcraft and Demonology.* New York: Crown, 1970.

Ross, Peter. *A History of Long Island.* New York: Lewis Pub. Co., 1902.

Russell, Jeffrey Burton. *Witchcraft in the Middle Ages.* Ithaca: Cornell University Press, 1972.

Seip, Elizabeth Cloud. "Witch-Finding in Western Maryland." Journal of American Folk-Lore, Vol. 47, 1934.

Shoemaker, Henry W. *The Origin and Language of Central Pennsylvania Witchcraft*. Reading: Eagle Press, 1927.

Simor, George. "Witchcraft Alive and Well and Living on Long Island." Paumanok, the Magazine of Long Island Living, Vol. 1, No. 1, June, 1973.

Smith, De Cost. "Witchcraft and Demonism of the Modern Iroquois." Journal of American Folk-Lore, Vol. 1, 1888.

Smith, Marion Whitney. *Algonquin and Abenaki Indian Myths and Legends*. Lewiston: Central Maine Press, 1962.

Smith, Susy. *Today's Witches*. Englewood Cliffs: Prentice-Hall, 1970.

Spade, Watt, and Walker, Willard. *Cherokee Stories*. Tahlequa, Okla.: [no pub. listed], 1966.

Steiner, Roland. "Observations on the Practice of Conjuring in Georgia." Journal of American Folk-Lore, Vol. 14, 1901.

Tallant, Robert. *Voodoo in New Orleans*. New York: Macmillan, 1946.

Underhill, Ruth Murray. *Red Man's America*. Chicago: University of Chicago Press, 1953.

———. *Red Man's Religion*. Chicago: University of Chicago Press, 1965.

Vogel, Virgil J. *American Indian Medicine*. Norman: University of Oklahoma Press, 1970.

Wallace, Ernest. "Some Explanatory Origins in Comanche Folklore." West Texas Historical Association Year Book, Vol. 23, Oct. 1947.

West, John Foster. *You Take the Highroad: Along the Blue Ridge Parkway*. Charlotte: Heritage Press, 1974.

Winsor, Justin (ed.). *The Memorial History of Boston*. Boston: James R. Osgood & Co., 1881.

Wissler, Clark. *Indians of the United States.* Garden City: Doubleday, 1966.

Worthen, Samuel Copp. "Witches in New Jersey and Elsewhere." New Jersey Historical Society Proceedings, New series, Vol. 8, 1923.

Archives of Maryland, Proceedings of the Council of Maryland, 1636–1637. Baltimore: Maryland Historical Society, 1885.

INDEX

Allyn, Thomas, 23
Antoine, Pére, 128
Aunt Sarah, 68

Baltimore, Lord, 64
Barker, George, 72
Barnes, Elizabeth, 74
Bassett, Goody, 22
Batts, Kate, 103, 106
Bazar, Joseph, 134
Bell, Allen, 100
Bell, Betsy, 100-101, 102-103, 104, 105, 107
Bell, Drew, 100
Bell, Joel, 100
Bell, John, 99-107
Bell, John (of Mississippi), 107-108
Bell, Mary, 107-109
Bell, William, 100

Bennett, Captain, 72
Bennett, Elizabeth, 65
Blackbeard (Capt. Edward Teach), 43-44
Black witch, defined, 17
Blymer, John, 174
Bonney, Anna, 86-87
Bosworth, Capt. John, 63-64
Buckland, Dr. Raymond, 170-171

Calvert, Charles, 65-66
Campbell, Caroline, 162
Campbell, Cornelius, 162-164
Capps, Richard, 74
Carrington, John, 21-22
Carver, Capt. William, 74
Chamberlayne, George, 32-39
Charles I (king of England), 13, 64

Index

Chata, 139-140
Chávez, Juan, 139-140
Chocorua, 161-165, 167
Clarke, Walter, 37
Cole, Ann, 25-26
Coleman, Joe, 84-85
Cowman, John, 65
Crispin, Granny, 56
Cromwell, Oliver, 64
Cunjering, defined, 79

Dean (Bell slave), 101, 106
Dédé (voodoo queen), 114-115, 128
Discovery of Witches, The (Hopkins), 13
Dr. Jack, 124-125
Dr. John, 119-124, 175
Dr. Yak-Yak, 124

Elizabeth I (queen of England), 12, 13
Ethelstan, 10
Exorcist, The (Blatty), 177

Gardiner, Lion, 91
Gardner, Joshua, 102, 105, 107
Garlick, Elizabeth, 91
Gilbert, John, 23-25
Gilbert, Lydia, 22-25
Gilbert, Thomas, 22-23
Gisburne, Jane, 74
Gisburne, John, 74
Glapion, Louis, 127-128, 131
Glapion, Marie, 135

Godby, Ann, 73
Goodale, Elizabeth, 65
Goya, 143
Grady, Katherine, 72
Greensmith, Nathaniel, 25-26
Greensmith, Rebecca, 25-26
Greye, Rebecca, 71
Gris-gris, 113

Haley, Capt. Sam, 43
Hall, Ralph, 92
Harding, William, 72
Harrison, John, 26
Harrison, Katherine, 26-27
Hendrickson, Yeshro, 60
Herrmann, James M., 175
Hex marks, 50
Hibbins, Ann, 20
Hopkins, Matthew, 13, 75
Howe, Elizabeth, 45
Howe, Nicholas, 29

Innocent VIII (Pope), 12

Jackson, Henry, 84-85
Jackson, Jane, 86-87
Jackson, Joe, 87
Jackson, Julia, 118
James I (king of England), 13
Jenkins, Jane, 74
Jenkins, Lazarus, 74
Jennings, Samuel, 37
Jesus, 58, 64
John. *See* Dr. John
Johnson, James, 102, 103

Johnson, Mary, 21
Johnson, William, 102
Jones, Laura, 84-85
Jones, Margaret, 20
Jones, Thomas, 20
Jung, Granny, 56

Kate (Bell servant), 102-103
Knapp, Goodwife, 22

Lala (voodoo queen), 116-118
Latour, Malvina, 135
Laveau, Marie, 125, 126-136
Lee, Mary, 63-64
Leek, Sybil, 170, 171
Lightfoot, Hosey, 85
Lujan, Manuel, 144-145
Luther, Martin, 12

Main, Harry, 45-48
Mansfield, George N., 97
Marshall, Bill, 83-84
Mather, Cotton, 19
Mather, Increase, 19
Mattson, Margaret, 60
McGahee, Hattie, 84-86
McGill, Granny, 55
McKay, Joseph M. (Dr. Cat),
   125
Moses, 9, 54-55, 58
Myers, Granny, 57

Nikki, 171
Nostradamus, 122

Paris, Jacques, 126

Parsons, Hugh, 20
Parsons, Mary (Northampton),
   21
Parsons, Mary (Springfield), 20
Penn, William, 60
Pilate, Pontius, 64
Pocahontas, 70
Powhatan (Algonquin chief),
   70
Prescott, Edward, 65

Rehmeyer, Nelson D., 174
Richardson, Elizabeth, 65
Rookens, Jane, 72
Rose, Nicholas, 29

Saloppé, Marie, 129
Sanford, Mary, 26
Scot, Captain, 44
Sherwood, Grace, 74-75
Sherwood, James, 74
Shimsky, Albert, 175
Smith, Capt. John, 69-70
Staples, Goodwife, 22
Starett, D. B., 97
Stiles, Henry, 23-24

Theodore of Tarsus, 10
Trimmings, Oliver, 29
Trimmings, Susannah, 28-29

Varlett, Judith, 26

Walford, Jane, 28-30
Walton, George, 33, 35, 36-40

Walton, William, 36
Warmoth, Henry Clay, 134
Washington, George, 65
Washington, John, 65
Werewolf, 146
West, John Foster, 97
White witch, defined, 17
Williams, Roger, 28
Wilson, George, 56
Winthrop, John, 21, 26, 91
Witch mark, 16
Witchcraft
    the American Indian and, 150-168; the Bell Witch (Mississippi), 107-109; the Bell Witch (Tennessee), 99-107; Brown Mountain, the lights of, 97-98; legend of Chocorua, 161-165; the Devil's Tramping Ground and, 94-96; European history of, 9-14; in Georgia, 78-87; history of, 14-18; Marie Laveau and, 125, 126-136; Lithobolia, legend of, 31-40; Harry Main's treasure, legend of, 45-48; in Maryland, 62-69; in Mississippi, 107-109; in New England, 19-30, 31-48; legends of New England, 31-48; in New Jersey, 88-89; in New Mexico, 137-149; in New Orleans, 111-125, 121-136; in New York, 90-92; in North Carolina, 89-90, 92-98; in Pennsylvania Dutch country, 49-61; Rhode Island and, 28; in Salem, Massachusetts, 19-20; in South Carolina, 90; Tennessee, 99-107; today, 169-177; in Virginia, 69-77; Voodoo, 111-125, 126-136; watching woman, legend of, 40-45
Wright, Jane, 70-71
Wright, Mary, 91

Yeardley, George, 70, 71
You Take the Highroad: Along the Blue Ridge Parkway (West), 97
Young, Alse, 21

ABOUT THE AUTHOR

Clifford Lindsey Alderman was born in Springfield, Massachusetts, and graduated from the United States Naval Academy at Annapolis. Much of his subsequent career was as an editor and in public relations work in the field of shipping and foreign trade, but during World War II he returned to naval service.

Mr. Alderman has written historical novels for adults and both fiction and nonfiction for young people. He believes in knowing firsthand the places of which he writes and has traveled extensively in Europe, Canada and the West Indies, and throughout the United States.

He lives with his wife in Seaford, New York.